Ruth Hall

In the brave Days of old

A Story of Adventure in the Time of King James the First

Ruth Hall

In the brave Days of old
A Story of Adventure in the Time of King James the First

ISBN/EAN: 9783337177195

Printed in Europe, USA, Canada, Australia, Japan

Cover: Foto ©ninafisch / pixelio.de

More available books at **www.hansebooks.com**

IN THE BRAVE DAYS OF OLD

A STORY OF ADVENTURE IN THE
TIME OF KING JAMES
THE FIRST

BY

RUTH HALL

BOSTON AND NEW YORK
HOUGHTON, MIFFLIN AND COMPANY
The Riverside Press, Cambridge
1898

COPYRIGHT, 1898, BY RUTH HALL.

ALL RIGHTS RESERVED.

TO
MY NEPHEWS
FOR WHOM IT WAS WRITTEN
THIS STORY IS
DEDICATED

PREFACE.

I HAVE chosen, for the period in which these scenes are laid, the ten years between the death of Queen Elizabeth and the first settlement at Manhattan.

It is a time seldom approached in fiction, and yet rich in notable personages and romantic adventures. It portrays the condition, at that date, of Europe and of America, and thus betrays the reasons which induced emigrants to leave their homes to begin life again in a new country. More than all, it shows the relations of the earliest colonies that dotted the shores of what are now the United States, and the conditions which governed them. That decade saw the true beginnings of a nation.

Because so much now depends upon what happened then, because our country rose to be what she is from what other countries were, I have written the adventures of two boys, three hundred years ago, for young Americans of the end of the nineteenth century.

CONTENTS

CHAPTER		PAGE
I.	THE DEATH-BED OF A QUEEN	1
II.	HOW THE NEWS REACHED HOLYROOD	11
III.	THE HOUSE ON THE MOOR	22
IV.	KING JAMES PASSES SENTENCE	33
V.	KIDNAPED	43
VI.	IN THE OAK ROOM	54
VII.	FROM THE TOWER TO WINCHESTER	67
VIII.	ENTER GUY FAWKES	79
IX.	THE GUNPOWDER PLOT	91
X.	AT HOLBEACH	101
XI.	PRINCE HENRY AND CAPTAIN SMITH	113
XII.	THE TOWN CLOCK AT SLUYS	124
XIII.	WITH PRINCE MAURICE	134
XIV.	KLAASZOON THE MARTYR	145
XV.	BEFORE GROLL	155
XVI.	THE RECORDER'S GUEST	165
XVII.	IN GIBRALTAR BAY	176
XVIII.	WHEN THE SMOKE CLEARED	186
XIX.	THE KING'S SWORD	195
XX.	ON THE HALF MOON	206
XXI.	TAKEN CAPTIVE	218
XXII.	WHAT HAPPENED ON HUDSON'S RIVER	230
XXIII.	WINONA'S TOTEM	243
XXIV.	THE VICTIM OF RAVAILLAC	256
XXV.	THE NORTHWEST PASSAGE	267
XXVI.	AN ARCTIC WINTER	279
XXVII.	MUTINY	290
XXVIII.	ADRIFT WITH HUDSON	302
XXIX.	FROM BAY TO RIVER	315
XXX.	YOUNG AMERICANS	325

IN THE BRAVE DAYS OF OLD

CHAPTER I

THE DEATH-BED OF A QUEEN

"GILES! art awake, Giles?"

It was a windy, rainy night in March. Giles Valentine sprang from his bed. A pebble had been thrown against the lattice. A voice called to him from the garden below. He ran to the window and thrust the sash aside. Through the dark he could make out a man's figure, — a figure holding a lighted lantern in one hand.

The boy leaned forward: "Who's there?"

"Hist!" said the man, raising his finger to his lip. "Canst climb from the window, Giles? I would not that the household be roused, but I need thee, lad."

It was the voice of Giles's guardian, and of the family's nearest neighbor, Sir Robert Carey. The idea of disobedience never entered the boy's head, and a thrill of pleasure ran through his veins at the chance of so mysterious an adventure.

"In one moment," he answered. "It shall not take long to dress. I can swing myself down by the vine and the laburnum. Wait only one moment."

"Haste!" was the reply. "Make haste!"

With nervous trembling, Giles hurried into his clothing. He threw his short cloak over his shoulder, and seized his plumed bonnet. At last he was ready. He cautiously crept upon the window-sill. As he thrust out one foot to find lodging in the stout ivy stalk nailed against the house, the man, waiting for him in the garden, called to him in the same hushed tones: —

"Hast money with thee, Giles?"

The boy paused, surprised, and looked down at him from his perch. "All I own," he answered, "is in my belt. I have" —

"No matter. Thy mother keeps thee well supplied. And art warmly wrapped? We may ride far to-night."

Much wondering what this could mean, Giles nodded assent, continuing his climb. It was an easy feat for a strong, nimble fellow used to the sport. He caught a surer foothold upon a swinging tree-branch, thus throwing himself from the vine to that support, and thence sliding quickly to the ground. Carey seized him at once by the shoulder.

"Now thy pony," he whispered in the boy's ear. "Have him at the park gate as speedily as may be. I shall wait thee there. Haste, lad. Thou canst not guess the need for haste. Thy whole future may depend on 't."

Puzzled indeed by these words, impressively delivered, the boy sped across the drawbridge, always down in these peaceful days of Queen Elizabeth. He dashed at a tangent over the bowling green, and disappeared from sight among the offices that clustered close to the Grange. When he reappeared, leading his pony over the grass-plots that there might be no sound, his guardian was nowhere to be seen. At the park gate they met again.

"Ride like the wind," commanded Carey, swinging himself to his own saddle. He gathered up the reins, and gave his horse the spur. "Follow me," he cried over his shoulder, "and ride like the wind!"

Nothing loth, Giles mounted, and slapped Dapple smartly with his palm. A delicious sensation of excitement and exultation possessed him.

"Lead on, sir," he called as his steed broke into a gallop. "I shall follow you."

On and on they rode, through the rough tracks that at that time were called the highroad, on and on, in a breathless silence, past leafless hedgerows, and here and there a silent house, sleeping in the quiet before the dawn. The pattering raindrops fell upon them. The raw cold crept through Giles's cloak and his close-fitting, lace-trimmed vest. The romance of this adventure was all he felt. He urged Dapple at the heels of his guardian's horse.

They entered Richmond. He began to question within himself if it could be possible that the palace was their destination. The queen lay ill, some men said dying, within that dusky pile of buildings that stretched out before them. Scattered lights gleamed in the casements. Carey glanced up towards one window with a face of such keen anxiety that Giles remarked the look.

"Not yet," the man muttered between his teeth.

He pulled up his horse by the roadside, beckoning the boy to come closer to him.

"Now it is your part," he said rapidly, bending over his saddle so that his face approached his ward's. "Giles, thou hast a friend among the queen's pages, — young Verrooy?"

"Oh, Jan? Yes, sir, I know Jan right well."

"Go thou to him at once. Seek him out, and tell him I would have speech with him without delay. He will doubtless plead duty. But all is confusion there. Her Majesty is nigh death. Tell him thou wilt take his place for the time, and I must speak with him."

"Ay," said Giles readily. "And then?"

Carey dropped his voice still lower. Giles saw that the hand laid on his saddle-bow was shaking. "Then thou must make thy way to the queen's apartments. Hush! — this is no time for parley. Do as I tell thee. Thou art a brave lad, and cunning. Thou must not be detected nor noted. But slip thyself in there *thou shalt*. Bring me word all that takes place; if the queen sinks or gains, and what is said about her. Thou must see her Majesty with thine own eyes, to tell me how she fares. No one will mark thee among the boys that wait upon her. And thou shalt behold " (he kept his keen glance upon Giles's reluctant face) " what many men would give one eye to witness, — the death-bed of Elizabeth."

With all the incentive of curiosity and of risk, it was not a task to Giles's liking. Still he had no notion of downright refusal to his guardian's demand. He threw his reins to Carey, and slid softly to the ground. Across the road he ran, watched his chance, and slipped unnoticed into the very doorway of the palace. As the man had surmised, all was unsettled there. Giles had never visited Jan before. He had never seen the queen, although she had appeared in public not long since. A question or two brought him to the presence of his friend. Two boys sat upon a bench in an antechamber, leaning against each other, blinking and rubbing their eyes.

It was a favorable moment for Carey's plan. Jan was but partially wakened by Giles's touch on his shoulder, and Giles's whisper in his ear. He met the proposition that the new-comer should take his place without the demur he would have made had he realized what it meant. The other attendant stretched his arms wide, smiled from one to the other, and threw his full length upon the bench. In an instant he was fast asleep. Jan looked at him enviously, yawned, and, with drooping eyelids and lagging step, sauntered away to the appointment.

Giles drew a long breath.

A heavy curtain hung across one door opposite to him. Behind this he could hear soft voices and hurried steps. Another door, near this, stood open.

Presently, through this last, a little procession came walking solemnly. Giles recognized the leader, a grave-faced man, in black velvet cap and gown. It was the secretary, Cecil.

A courtier glanced towards the seat where Giles was watching with earnest eyes. The boy's heart gave a leap. The man motioned to him. Here was his opportunity. He sprang to his feet. This was the queen's Council, he was sure, and they were going to the death-bed. Giles sped across the room. He pulled the curtain aside. He stood back to watch the company file through the doorway. Then in their shadow he entered the royal presence.

An enormous, high-canopied bedstead stood in the centre of the apartment. Beside it, on the rich Turkey rug, knelt weeping women.

A physician, glass in hand, stood at the headboard. On the white pile of pillows, — one of the luxuries of that day, — lay the mighty queen. Giles could not take his eyes from her.

It was an old, old woman that he saw: she seemed even older than her years. Her streaming locks had the peculiar ashy appearance of light hair turned gray. Her features were sharply drawn. Her nose and mouth had a peevish, pinched expression. Her hazel eyes looked out wistfully from her pale face, as if they tried to speak.

The secretary approached her bed. He bent the knee reverently.

"Madam," he said, "your faithful servants have returned for some sure token of your Majesty's will. One hour ago," — he kept watch of those speaking eyes, — "we asked whose was the succession. You answered us: 'No rascal's son, but a king's.' Your gracious Majesty knows what this means to the land you will leave comfortless. We pray you make your wishes plain. Who is to rule? Is it to be James of Scotland?"

Every eye in the room was fixed upon her now. Giles suddenly felt assured that this was his errand. He remembered boasts from

Carey of his patron in Edinburgh. The answer of Elizabeth was what he was to carry to his guardian.

She tried to speak again and again. No articulate sound could force its way through the shrunken lips. At last — it seemed an endless time — she slowly, painfully raised her two hands, those beautifully shaped hands that princes were wont to praise. Above her head they crept. Over her forehead they formed a crown.

"It is King James," said Cecil.

Giles left the room, no one heeding nor hindering. He hastened noiselessly past Jan's slumbering comrade, through the passages to the outer air. He found his friend, covered by Carey's cloak, asleep on the dry grass where the horses were stamping restlessly close at hand. His guardian sprang from out the shadow.

"Well?" he breathed.

Giles told his story in the fewest words. He saw Carey's face light up. His hand tightened upon the hilt of his sword. "As I hoped and believed," he cried. "Lad, lad, our fortunes are made!"

Still he did not remove his gaze from the building. His eyes were fastened upon the light within one window, in no little anxiety and impatience.

The casement moved. Carey flung his rein to the boy. He sprang across the road. A lady's head appeared in the lighted square. It bent forward. A white hand threw *something* to the watcher below. He seized it, looked, and then made one bound towards the nearest door. He glanced inside.

Back he came, like a shadow. He scrambled into his saddle, and motioned in agitation to Giles. He thrust one hand into his doublet. The boy saw that it held a glistening ring.

"Turn," he hissed, "and ride as thou never hast before! Our fortunes are made, I tell thee, Giles. Elizabeth is dead, and thou and I — we shall carry the news to King James."

CHAPTER II

HOW THE NEWS REACHED HOLYROOD

"My poor Giles," said Sir Robert, looking back as he rode. "Thou art nigh done for, art thou not?"

His ward drew a long, gasping breath. He was bent forward upon the pommel. One stiff hand loosened itself from the rein. The other reached out to return Carey's kindly touch. It was seldom that anything in the nature of a caress was given to him by this stern, quiet man. The boy, thoroughly exhausted by this ceaseless exertion, was much affected. He said quickly, though his tone showed the fatigue he would not acknowledge: —

"Methinks I shall be myself again when I have had a good night's sleep. It is the change from one relay of horses to another that tires me most. With Dapple, I could stand as long a ride, I know."

"'T is the night work," observed Sir Robert. "Thou art full young for such an enterprise, yet thou hast proven thyself a man. Courage! We shall reach Edinburgh to sup and rest. We shall" —

The horse made a misstep. His tired rider was off his guard, sitting carelessly. He pitched forward, fell heavily over the animal's head, and at full length in the roadway. In an instant Giles was upon the ground. He knelt beside the prostrate figure that remained without movement or word.

"Sir, speak to me!" implored the boy. "Tell me, are you sorely hurt, and where? Oh, what shall I do? what shall I do?"

Blood streamed down the man's ghastly face from a long wound under his curling hair. Giles wrung his hands, looking about him to search the landscape for a sign of help. Since they left Norham Castle behind them that day, they had met few fellow wayfarers. None was visible now. There was no habitation in sight. He felt utterly at a loss.

Without the slightest warning, Sir Robert started to his feet. He staggered like a drunken man, and leaned heavily upon his ward. But his blood-stained features were set in determination.

"Help me to mount," was all he said.

"Oh, sir, you cannot. See! you know not how you are hurt. You falter"—

"Help me to mount."

The boy shook his head in perplexity and distress. He settled his guardian in the saddle, and handed him the reins.

"You cannot hold out," he began, despairingly. "You must wait"—

"I tell thee I will not wait! Until we reach Holyrood I can hold out, and I will."

Five hours later, the guards who stood before the king's bedchamber were startled by an unwonted sight. A travel-worn stranger, white as death, with blood upon his face, half led by a trembling boy, pushed through their ranks imperiously.

"Make way for word from London!" he cried.

He thrust back their protests. He was past them, dragging his ward with him. Again Giles entered a royal presence.

It was a dreary waste of room, poorly furnished, lighted by candles that betrayed, it must be confessed, no little dirt as well as poverty. In a high-backed, richly carved chair sat the only occupant of this immense apartment. He was dressed in a thickly wadded suit of hunters'-green clothes that were the worse for wear and not scrupulously clean. His figure was tall and slender, with spindling legs that seemed too slight to support his body. His eyes were prominent and staring. When he spoke, it was hard for Giles to understand him, so Scotch were his phrases and so indistinct was his voice.

Carey threw himself on his knees before him. Seizing one hand, he pressed it to his lips.

"Hail, James," he said, "King of England and Scotland!"

"Is't true? Is't true, mon?" queried his sovereign, pulling Carey towards him. He looked up into the man's face, then averted his eyes quickly, patting the arm he grasped. "Is't true, then? Is she deid?"

"Your gracious Majesty," Carey replied, "it is quite true."

"How dost ken?"

"Lady Scrope flung this ring" — he held it out — "from the window, as we had agreed, for a token. I glanced into one room, at random. The women were all weeping together. Then I took horse and rode, at once, and night and day, to you. I was resolved that you should hear this from no one else, ere I had kept my word."

"Ay, ay," James nodded. "'T was well done. Thou hast long since engaged to bring me back the ring when Elizabeth should depart hence. When was 't, good Carey?"

"On Thursday, your Majesty."

"Thursday?" His dull face lighted up. "That is the Tudor day. Henry died on Thursday, and Mary, and Edward, and now Elizabeth. But, Carey" — he gazed wistfully at the other, stroking his arm more coaxingly — "said she aught of me?"

Carey was prepared for this question. He beckoned Giles to come forward.

"This lad, an' it please your Majesty," he said, "can tell what happened at the deathbed, and in what express terms her Majesty's royal cousin was named."

Giles was a handsome little fellow. His rosy cheeks and waving chestnut locks commended him to a monarch partial to pretty boys. The king's eyes glittered as he listened to the story. In a few bashful words that scene by the bedside of the English Semiramis was described, to the delight of the auditor. James hesitated. This was the happiest moment of his life. Yet he hated to part with anything that belonged to him. Slowly he drew from his finger the sapphire ring Carey had brought him and held it out to Giles.

"Take this, bonny wee mon," said he, "and tell me more of thee. Who art thou, laddie?"

"Giles Valentine, your Majesty. My father was killed in the Low Countries. My mother is Margaret Valentine, of the Grange nigh Richmond."

"Art a good son, Giles?"

"I strive to be. This gentle"—he bowed to Carey—"is my guardian. He knows."

"He is the best of lads," Carey said heartily. "And he stood this fearful ride like a hero."

Possibly the speaker was not averse from reminding the king what a ride it had been. But James shunned the subject, as he shunned the sight of Carey's wound. Blood was morbidly abhorrent to him, and the thought of obligation was none too strong.

"Gave thy mother permission that thou shouldst do this thing?" he inquired sharply of Giles in his thick-tongued Scotch.

"Your Majesty, I had no time to ask it. My guardian bade me, and I came. He sent word to my home that I was with him, and safe. It was the best that I could do."

"And why bring the lad?" asked the king.

Carey explained. He wished an eyewitness of Elizabeth's design, and he felt that the message he carried was too valuable to trust to one person, with the accidents that might befall.

"We have a good son," said the Scotch king, breaking in on Sir Robert's speech, and addressing Giles. "We have two laddies. Thou shalt see Baby Charles. But Prince Henry — Ah, he is my heart's jewel! — he is with the Earl of Mar. Some day, wee mon, some day, long, long to come, he shall rule over thee and thine, shall our son, as Henry the Ninth."

He started from his chair. "Ring the bell, ring the bell!" he cried imperiously to Carey. "And begone, good sirs. I love ye kindly. I — I shall not forget ye. But now I must see my queen. We shall put ye in the care of those," he glanced askance at Carey's face, "who will tend to your injuries."

Thus dismissed, Giles and his guardian backed themselves from the presence.

Carey was immediately seized upon by a group of courtiers, who guessed his errand and were desirous of hearing the particulars.

Giles was addressed by a youth some years his elder, clad in shabby and outgrown clothing. His thin features had a ferret-like expression. His small eyes were sly. He linked their arms together, introducing himself as a fellow countryman of the name of George Earl. He led Giles into the dining-hall, throwing aside a threadbare curtain of tarnished gold, and ushering his companion to the welcome sight of a spread table.

Giles made a hearty meal of the coarse food, while George plied him with questions. He not only soon learned the two messengers' tidings, but also what Giles could tell him of his family and himself. The proudest fact in the boy's short life was soon related:—

"My father was with the Lord High Admiral on the Triumph. He fought in the Channel against the Armada of Spain."

George gave a little cry of surprised admiration. Giles thrust one hand beneath his vest and unbuckled the belt he always wore under it about his waist. George's small eyes twinkled covetously, as he watched the other turn the pocket of soft leather inside out, and the tiny heap of coins that fell jingling to the board. Among them was a medal.

"It was struck in Holland," explained

Giles, pushing it forward. "On one side thou seest Philip's ships in order. Then there is the date, 1588, and the motto, 'Flavit et dissipati sunt.'"

"What is the reverse?" asked George, weighing the medal in his palm.

"The church on a rock, surrounded by stormy waves," Giles answered. "And the motto, 'Allidor non Laedor.' I value that medal next to my father's sword."

He opened his lips to point out to George the initials A.V. scratched lightly in the sail of one of the engraved ships. At that moment they were interrupted by Carey.

Official word had arrived, he said, from London. They themselves had not many hours' start of this courier, who was raging to find that Elizabeth's death was already known. King James intended to bid farewell to his people in the church. All the court were to attend that service on Sunday.

Giles felt deeply the impressiveness of the scene. James, with Anne of Denmark by his side, stood in his place surrounded by weeping folk who pressed forward to touch his hand. It was like a father's leave-taking from his children. There was something homely about it, presenting a worthier view of the often misjudged man who was England's new ruler.

In about ten days he left Edinburgh for the border. Again a curious picture was presented to the onlooker. In the streets, a gaping crowd about him, the king kissed his wife and bade her good-by for a season. She was to follow with their children a few weeks later.

George had struck up a rather one-sided friendship with the Englishmen who were to make part of James's train. While the two lads rode side by side together, he was voluble in his joy that his face was turned homeward again. "I came to Holyrood," he explained, "a year since with my uncle. I have pined for Warwick each day of that year. Wist thou, Giles, that Archie was mine uncle?"

Archie was the court fool.

"Nay," said Giles, marveling that George spoke as if this were some honor. "Thou hast told me naught of it."

He felt vaguely that he should be kinder to George for this discovery. When they made their first halt at night, the younger men and boys were quartered, after the rudest fashion, in outhouses, sleeping upon piles of straw or their own cloaks. Giles would have preferred biding by his guardian, or, since that could not be, by some one of the steadier young Scotchmen. Still he would not hurt George by any avoidance, and George kept close to him.

The morning dawned raw and gloomy. Giles rose betimes, that he might bathe and dress before the others. He felt at once that his belt was loosely hanging at his side. He ran his fingers along its surface. It was exactly as he feared.

The pocket was empty. His money and medal were gone.

CHAPTER III

THE HOUSE ON THE MOOR

CAREY did not give his ward much sympathy when Giles found him out to tell him of his loss.

"'T is of no avail trying to trace it," he said, "among all these strangers. In time thou mayst discover the medal. I do not wish to raise a hue and cry with the Scotchmen. They have no love for us as it is. It would go hard with thee, I fear me, shouldst thou accuse them of theft."

Giles looked very sober. "I know not what my mother will say," quoth he, "when I return to her without the medal."

"It may come to light ere this progress is done," Carey suggested. "Cheer thee, lad. There are worse losses than thine. What thinkst thou his Majesty announced but now?"

Giles had no idea.

"He has given thee nothing for thy ride to him. Nothing, Giles. For me, I am to be gentleman of the bedchamber. A fine office, forsooth! Gentleman of the bedchamber for all my reward!"

The boy began to speak.

"Hush," whispered Carey, busying himself about the harness of his horse. "Say nothing. Yon comes young Earl. I trust not that fox-faced varlet. Men tell me that Archie the fool coveted this new post of mine, poor though it be, for George's brother in the Mid-Counties."

George hung about the younger boy persistently, in this long drawn-out Southern journey. Giles had no less suspicion of him than his guardian felt. He endeavored to shun George whenever he could quietly do so. Sometimes he felt that his schemes for avoidance were guessed and resented.

The monotonous round of country gayety and entertainment was drawing to a close. They had entered upon the last half of the tour. One afternoon of a mild spring day Giles found himself riding alone, having fallen behind the train of horsemen. Twilight was closing in. They were to stop for the night, he knew, with a gentleman called Sir Oliver Cromwell. Giles jogged slowly along the rough road, absorbed in thought: of the odd life he was leading, of his recent loss, of his mother, his little sister Meg, of Jan, and what he might be doing.

Suddenly there was a tremendous crash. His horse stumbled, pitching upon his knees. Giles was thrown violently over his head. He fell, apparently, from a considerable height. Confused ideas rushed through his mind. Then everything became black before him, and he knew nothing more.

When the boy recovered consciousness, it was in the dusk of the long afterglow. About him stretched what looked like an unending black wall. He gazed up a distance of ten or twelve feet before he could see the branches of trees etched against the clear sky.

He felt each limb cautiously, putting his hand to his head. There was no wound anywhere. When he finally staggered to his feet, he saw that, shaken though he was, no bones were broken by the fall. He was evidently in a deep pit. Doubtless, his horse had wandered from the track; he, busy with recollections of home, had not noticed this. The hole was some rude excavation, common in that rough country, and a serious sort of mantrap when the captured had no comrade at liberty to extricate him.

Giles seated himself again, to think over calmly what was to be done. His riderless steed might never find the others. In a strange land, it would be curious if he chanced to fall in with the king's men, or be recognized by any one. Carey would miss his charge in time, although not, very possibly, until several days had gone by, and until the company were far advanced upon their way again. He saw little of the boy, during these interrupted times of constant change. None of the others would be interested to institute a search for him, unless George Earl should do so. And Giles had his doubts of George's friendship.

No, it was manifest that there was no reliance to be placed upon any outside help. He must try to save himself, or — Giles did not like to dwell upon the alternative. He might linger here, in this dismal hole, scorched by the sun, beaten upon by the rain, whipped by the winds, till, worn out by exposure and the torture of hunger and thirst, he died, and his bones were found, at some distant hour, to tell the tale, if aught remained for recognition, to his mother and little Meg.

Yet all about him the dark walls rose,

sheer, without a break. It was like a shallow well. There was no foothold anywhere by which he could scramble even part way towards the surface of the ground.

What should he do?

After carefully examining the pit, Giles began to consider its outer resources. On the brink of the descent was a stout sapling. It was thus temptingly close at hand, and yet far away, at least six feet from the outstretched fingers of the boy when standing on tiptoe. It would give a support to a pulley, he mused, looking up at it longingly. Ah, he had an inspiration!

Unwinding the long, silken sash from about his waist, he tore it lengthwise in two. It was stout, requiring his dirk to cut it, but he was glad of this, for it showed the strength of the stuff. There were a few loose stones upon the rocky bottom of the pit. He tied one of these within the fringe of his sash. Aided by the clearness of the light, and by the rising moon, he began his efforts to escape.

Over and over again he made the attempt, throwing the loaded, improvised rope, so that one end should surround the tree trunk and fall back within the hole, while he still held the other in his left hand. Over and over he failed, until, if the experiment had not been so desperate, he should have given it up in despair. This was life or death, so Giles put forth another effort, and another, and another.

Sometimes the silken sling fell far short of the tree. Sometimes it went around it, as it should, but did not return to him in his prison. He tried again and again, his arm aching and his sight failing from excessive fatigue.

It was a desperate, not a deliberate aim that finally achieved what he had so long attempted in vain. Almost at random Giles made a careless fling. To his astonishment there fell at his feet the entangled end of silk while its middle encircled the tree trunk. He had a ladder ready to his hand.

He tied the two pieces together, pulling hard upon them. They stood the strain perfectly, and the sapling, though it swayed, was strong. Hand over hand Giles pulled himself up the rock. He was bruised against it. The young tree shook, and jarred him with its trembling. The distance was slight, after all. It was the work of a few moments to climb out from this treacherous spot. With a sensation of intense thankfulness, Giles felt the grass brush his cheek. He drew up his knees, and his feet touched the earth. He was safe.

He left the sash dangling upon the tree. Perhaps it would serve for a danger signal for some other traveler. And here the question confronted him, Where should he find shelter for the night? All about him lay a bleak expanse of waste land. Darkness was settling down upon the dreary scene, only relieved by the crescent moon. Far as the eye could see there was no sign of human being or of house. He walked forward at a venture, stumbling towards what he thought was the direction of the road, straining his sight to catch the glimmer of a light through the deepening gloom.

Was that a spark or a tiny star low on the horizon? No. Yes. It was a distant flicker of fire or candle, and it meant some companionship, at least.

On and on Giles ran towards that point of light, quickening his steps when the hunger he was beginning to feel pricked him forward, slowing his pace when his tired feet refused to keep up longer. It seemed hours before the light grew more distinct. By and by it resolved itself into a glow that came from one side of a long, low building. He was approaching some sort of house. He was impressed by the meanness of the surroundings, the unkempt ground, the tumbled-down aspect of the thatched hut, — for it was nothing more, — while he drew close to the window and peered within.

A bit of oiled paper answered the purpose of a pane. The rickety shutter hung half off. Inside the room into which Giles looked sat a beetle-browed, cadaverous man, clad in rusty finery, brooding over the fire, the only light in the room. A saddle of rich workmanship lay upon the mud floor. A broken chair or two, a stool for a table, seemed to comprise the furniture. Upon the stool sat a flagon and the remains of a meat pasty. Towards this last Giles gazed lovingly. He stole around to the door and knocked.

"Who is there?" called a gruff voice.

"One Giles Valentine," answered the boy. "A lad from the king's retinue who has lost his way and craves a night's lodging."

There was an exclamation of surprise. A bolt slipped, the door opened upon the crack. The beetle-browed man looked out.

"Art alone, then?" he demanded.

"Alone, good sir, and lost."

"Enter," was the churlish invitation.

Giles squeezed through the narrow opening, his host still holding the door. He walked into the house.

"What's this tale of thine?" said the man, bolting the entrance again, and looking the boy over from head to foot.

Giles related his mishap in detail. When he had finished, the man waved one hand towards the table. "There canst thou eat," said he. "And there," he pointed to a pallet covered with a riding-cloak in the obscurity of a corner, "there canst thou pass the night."

This surly hospitality was thankfully received. Giles refreshed himself, while his host, reseated by the fire, so far unbent as to question him minutely in regard to the royal progress. Such interest was so natural that Giles felt no hesitancy in telling him whatever he wanted to know.

He was dead tired and soon craved permission to seek the bed. The man, he fancied, rather hurried him into it. In spite of his fatigue there was something in the situation that kept the boy from sleep. Yet he saw the man by the fire cast so many sharp glances towards his corner that he soon shut his eyes, breathing slowly and heavily, to see what would come of this.

He heard a sigh of relief. Very soon he detected a light tap upon the window. The man heard it too. He sprang up, and, moving on tiptoe, stole softly outside the house. Giles could catch the murmur of conversation. Presently the man returned and the door was secured. There was a subdued tinkle and jingle, as of coins carefully handled. He dared not open his eyes.

A hushed silence followed. He could hear the crackle of the fire and the squeaking of the rickety chair. A loud noise broke the stillness: the trample of horses' feet, a pounding upon the door. Giles leaped from the bed, the man from his chair.

"Open in the king's name!"

The man dragged himself slowly to the door. He moved the bolt and it flew back from without. A mob fell into the room. Giles recognized them all. Carey was among their number. The foremost placed one hand upon the arm of his host.

"John Simon," he said, "thou art my prisoner."

It was all over in an instant. The boy found himself at his guardian's side. Before them on the stool lay an open wallet, from which a few coins had fallen. Carey picked up one, looked at it, and again more sharply.

He handed it to Giles. "Here, lad," he said, "however thou camest here, thou wert upon the track of thine own. See this."

It was the Dutch medal.

CHAPTER IV

KING JAMES PASSES SENTENCE

Giles could only look his astonishment at his guardian.

"Who is he?" he inquired, while they were swept with the crowd outside of the room. "Why is he apprehended?"

Sir Robert caught his bridle from a waiting groom. "Thou canst ride with me," he said. "Here, step on the stirrup and clasp me round the waist. As we go thou shalt tell me how thou cam'st in that den of thieves. Afterwards I will give thee the history of what has happed since I saw thee last at daybreak."

Giles accordingly mounted behind his guardian. He related his adventures in all haste, so eager was he to hear the other's story. Carey, too, made quick work of his news. For some days different members of the royal train had been complaining of losses. Money and jewels — such money and such jewels as the poor Scots possessed — had been stolen.

Last night the growing agitation over this mysterious pilfering had in some fashion reached the king's ears. He declared that the thief must be found, and must be made an example. A few hours since, two courtiers were stopped and robbed while riding by themselves along a lonely bit of road. Their description of the offender identified him with a notorious highwayman, to Sir Oliver Cromwell's mind. It was guessed that this Simon might have been following the company for the past week, and might be the scoundrel whose iniquities could now be brought home to him.

"Thy medal will go far to convict him," Sir Robert observed.

"Oh, sir, must it be so?" Giles grew pale. "'T was pilfered ere we left Scotland"—

"Surely," said his guardian in amazement, "thou wouldst not shield the fellow?"

"'T is not that; but he gave me shelter when I was in need. I would not be the one to harm him in return."

"Hush thy folly," was the stern response. "Justice waits not on thy concerns. Leave this in my hands. And here we are at Huntingdon."

A massive pile rose before them in the moonlight. The house stood in the midst of an irregularly laid-out park, where sheep and horses grazed by day among the trees, with which the meadow-land was sprinkled.

As Giles slid from the horse to the ground, a hand came out of the darkness and seized his arm. He was dragged away from his guardian, away from the group about the doorway, into the deeper shadow of an immense cedar.

"Spy!" a hoarse voice hissed in his ear. "Thou cowardly spy!"

"Who calls me spy?" cried the boy indignantly. "He who hides in the gloom and draws me from the presence of witnesses? Does he call me coward and spy?"

"I tell thee thou art a cur." Now he knew it for the utterance of George Earl, though it shook with passionate anger. "Thou art a cur. Thou hast sought out one who was good to thee, only that thou mightest lead these human bloodhounds there. Thou hast cause to be proud of thy work, Giles Valentine!"

"Giles Valentine!" called some one, like an echo.

Both lads started and looked whence the sound came. A man stood in the open doorway of the great house, his figure outlined against the light that streamed from within.

"Giles Valentine," he cried. "The king hath need of Giles Valentine."

With a heavy heart the reluctant witness came forward to the steps. He paid no heed to George, whom he heard following close behind. Up the broad entrance-way went the twain, past the man at the door, and so inside the hall.

It was a superb apartment which lay before them. The hall was some forty-five feet long, with height and breadth in proportion. A monstrous fire burned in the chimney opposite them. The dark wall was hung with gloomy portraits. A winding, enormously broad staircase led to the gallery above.

Before the fire, upon a sort of dais, sat King James in a chair hung with tapestry. Beside the platform was stationed the master of the house, a large-framed, strong-featured man, who held a little boy by the hand. The prisoner stood before them, and a clerk who was taking notes of a witness's evidence.

When it pleased him to lay aside his state, James the First was the most familiar of monarchs. He looked up at Giles's entrance, nodding affably to him.

"Here is our bonny mon," quoth he. "Come, Giles, laddie, and tell us thy story.

Sir Robert says that thou hast evidence to hang yon wretch."

Giles sickened at the words, which the sullen prisoner, in an attitude of obstinate pride, affected not to hear. The boy's white face and anxious eyes attracted the attention of the small son of the house. He pulled himself away from Sir Oliver to run to Giles.

" Poor lad," he said. " Has the naughty king frighted thee? I'll tell my father to chide him, an' thou sayest the word."

There was a broad laugh, led by the easy-going sovereign.

" Well spoken, my brave young Oliver," he exclaimed. " Thou hast a spirit beyond thy years. Would that our Charles," and he sighed, " who must be nigh as old as thee, had thy vigor and thy mind."

More than forty years afterwards, when Giles Valentine was growing to be an old man, the death of Charles recalled to his mind those words of King James. He thought how little his Majesty guessed that he was speaking to one who was to be instrumental in destroying that dear son of his.

" Come hither to me, laddie," called James. " Look at this mass of stuff." He indicated a pile of money and trinkets on the table between him and Sir Oliver. "Kenst thou aught of these?"

Giles took his courage in both hands. He sank on his knees at the platform's edge.

"May it please your Majesty," he began, "the man gave me food and lodging this night. Must I return his kindness with such foul ingratitude?"

"Good Giles," said King James earnestly, "when public ends are to be served, private matters must not be weighed against them. Majesty has learned that lesson, — and 't is bitter hard, my mon, — as all must learn it some time who come in contact with public doings. We are parts of a whole, laddie, — I and thou alike. Consider the whole and not the part. And now tell us if thou seest aught familiar in this collection, and if thou canst identify it without handling or coming nearer."

"Yon Dutch medal," said Giles slowly, pointing while he spoke, " I think to be mine, and so shall know it by one sign. 'T was my father's. He scratched the letters A. V. in the farther sail upon the right of the fleet."

The king examined the coin, handing it afterwards to Sir Oliver. The latter bowed gravely.

"Now tell us," James continued in the same gentle tone, "where thou lost thy token, and when."

Giles did so. His beseeching glance made the king inquire his further wish.

"May I go now, your Majesty?" he asked. "Am I needed longer?"

He was stifling, his head whirling, and his heart beating fiercely. It was impossible to tarry here in the glare of light and heat, to hear the man who had befriended him doomed to punishment, no matter how deserved.

James gave his permission, seeing how ill the boy looked, and perhaps fearing a complete breakdown. Suffering of any sort was always shunned by this Stuart.

Giles pushed through the throng to the stairway. He had some notion of seeking Sir Robert, who was not in the hall, and of hiding himself for the remainder of the night from sight or sound. Little Oliver again ran after him, grasping him by the coat. His father had given him directions in a hasty aside. The child — he was not yet five years old — had a manly expression upon his small, ugly face.

"I'll show thee where thou art to sleep," he said, leading the way up the stairs. "I'll take thee to the turret-room and make thee snug. Grieve not, good boy. Naught can harm thee whilst thou art with me."

Giles smiled sadly at the brag. Leaning over the railing, gaping down at the commotion below, was Archie, the court fool. He straightened himself and glared at the approaching pair. His deep-set eyes were wild with rage.

"Thou shalt pay dear for thy medal!" he muttered while they passed.

What could it all mean, thought Giles, — this intense interest shown by George and Archie in the fate of a common thief? Why their fury against him for the unwilling part he had been obliged to play?

Little Oliver kept his word. He found his guest a comfortable bed upon the floor of an antechamber. "Within there," said he, pointing to a larger room, " Sir Robert Carey sleeps. So my father bade me tell thee. Thou shalt be near thy friend. And now, good-night to thee; good-night and pleasant dreams."

This was a mockery, however well it was meant. Giles tossed upon his lowly couch the whole night long, seeking some respite from the tormenting remembrance of his testimony, of its probable consequences, and of the ill-will shown him by so powerful an enemy as the king's jester and prime favorite.

With the first streak of dawn he was upon his feet. Making a hasty toilet, he noiselessly left the room and sought egress from the house, feeling that the sweet, keen spring air of out of doors might drive away the blinding ache of his head, the result of a wakeful night and the accompaniment to an aching heart.

He threaded his course through many winding passages, by countless closed doors, to the great staircase which led down to the hall. Here a sleepy servant was just kindling the fire. He let the boy out of the door, with much clanking of bolt and chain.

Giles stood for a moment, his hand to his head, upon the step, uncertain which path to take for his stroll in the park. Something caught his eye: a figure lying face downward in the grass. He ran towards it.

George Earl lifted a tear-stained face to meet his pitying gaze. With a scream of aversion he jumped to his full height.

"Dost thou dare approach me?" he cried shrilly. "Thou viper! Away! Away, and rue the day thou thus repaid my brother's offer of a roof to thee, O thou hound of mischief!"

"Thy brother?" gasped Giles, a light breaking in upon him.

"Yes, wretch, my only brother, known by many names besides our father's. Hast come to gloat upon thy deed? Look there!"

His shaking hand was uplifted towards the woods back of the house. Giles wheeled about mechanically in the same direction. A horrid sight was thus revealed.

The trees, in their earliest dress of green, stood out against the sunrise. From a branch of an old oak-tree, in the pitiless light, was dangling the body of a man. They had hanged John Earl who called himself John Simon, to show how the new king was minded to deal with miscreants such as he.

CHAPTER V

KIDNAPED

It was useless to say a word to George. He only became the more infuriated with any effort towards sympathy or explanation. At the attempt he broke into horrible threats, of which Giles would have made light, had it not been for the recollection of Archie's malevolent salutation of the night before.

It was best to lay the whole affair before Sir Robert's superior judgment, the boy considered, and bent his steps towards the house once more.

That worthy gave a prolonged whistle when Giles had sought him out in his room. "The fool is, in truth, a formidable foe," he observed ruefully. "Be on thy guard, lad, and watch. Thou mayst receive, on the sudden, a signal to be gone."

He pondered the matter while he was dressing.

"Great festivities are preparing for to-day," he said. "There is to be one of those hunting parties, in which his Majesty delights. Presents will be offered him, and the peasantry round about will fling up the cap and shout for the king. We have become wonted to the particulars of a progress, have we not? They say Sir Oliver is to outdo all our other hosts. 'T will be hard in the bustle and hurry to find time to lay out a course of action. And yet" — Sir Robert laid down the sword he was buckling at his side, and glanced apprehensively toward his ward. He would not say the words, yet Giles understood his further thought: the busy, noisy day would be the time of times for the carrying out of a private grudge. How should he guard the boy?

Whenever it proved possible, they kept side by side throughout the morning. Sir Robert, who was more alarmed for Giles than Giles was for himself, did not allow his ward to go out of his sight. A banquet took up part of the day, — a meal of which one feature awakened the admiration of even these much-entertained Scotchmen. Two roasted boars stood in the middle of the table, harnessed to a mammoth plum pudding that had been made in the form of a wagon.

A presentation of gifts followed the feast,

after which the hunt was announced to take place in the park. Giles's horse had been traced and recovered since the previous day. He ran to the stables to see to its preparation. His courage asserted itself. His natural high spirits were rising; subdued though he felt by the highwayman's fate, he was now disposed to make sport of his relatives' revenge.

A groom hastened down from the house behind him, the steed he was leading trotting briskly.

"Is't Master Valentine?" asked the man.

"Yes," said Giles.

"This is for you, then."

He handed him a feather.

Stout though the boy's heart was, it stopped in its regular beat at the sight of this symbol. He understood its significance well. It meant flight.

"Whence came this token?" he demanded abruptly.

The servant scratched his head, a dull, hopeless expression crossing his face.

"I know not the gentles," he began slowly. "How can I tell who it might be? 'T was a fine, gay sir, in a velvet coat, the very color of an oak leaf in November."

Sir Robert had been dressed in that rich

red-brown to-day, but so had others of the train, — Archie, Giles quickly recalled, with the rest.

"A tall, dark man?" he inquired.

"Yes. No. Upon my honor, sir, I cannot say. I marked him not."

Was it a true warning, or was it a trap? In the first event every moment was precious.

"Sent he aught of message?" he finally asked.

"Good young sir, forgive me. Yes. He said you were to wait for him at the postern gate, and he would tell you more."

Giles must risk all, then. He must speed to the appointed place, and see what came of the meeting.

The man led out his horse. "I shall be prepared," he thought. "Neither friend nor foe shall take me by surprise."

It was a weary time — so it appeared to his agitated mind — that he paced Brown Bess up and down before the wicket; under the trees, out into the sun, back to the shadow again, and so under the trees.

A low whistle echoed through the woods. Involuntarily Giles turned his head in the direction of the sound. Like a flash of lightning some one clutched him from behind and dragged him from the saddle. He struggled vainly. His limbs were tightly pinioned. He was thrown to the ground. A huge bag was drawn over his head. He felt himself lifted between two persons, who caught him by the shoulders and the feet. He was placed upon a horse's back, roughly bound to the saddle, and there followed the racking motion of the animal urged to a brisk canter.

Nothing was said. Everything was done in perfect stillness. Giles could hear the quick beat of horse's hoofs beside the one he rode. When his ear became accustomed to the sounds, he felt certain that he had two attendants, one upon each side, either of whom placed a hand upon him from time to time, to steady the swaying sack which held him imprisoned. His head was raised against the pommel so high that there was no rush of blood. His brain was calm, despite the anguish he suffered in his uncomfortable position. His thoughts flew here and there like frightened birds.

He had no doubt that his captors were Archie and George. He resigned himself to inevitable torture, such as their hatred could devise. And would they dare to kill him?

He was by no means sure of this. He was,

in a sense, under the protection of King James. His guardian was of the royal household. Yet whatever they could do, — those enemies of his, — that, he knew, would be tried.

It was not long, although it seemed an age, before his doubts were changed to certainty. His horse was pulled to a halt. The straps that bound him to it were loosened. The sack was lifted to the ground. He was once more picked up, carried a few steps, and then — He was thrown from the height of several feet, and fell upon a bed of rock and stones. For an instant the agony was extreme, but the quick-witted boy realized that no bones were broken, and the cuts and bruises, he speedily reflected, were nothing in comparison with the fate which might have met him at those cruel hands. He heard the horses in retreat. He waited and waited for any other sound. No. It was evident that he had been left alone.

The full intention of the plot burst upon him. The whole had been cunningly devised. He never could accuse the jester and his nephew of the attack. He had neither seen them nor heard them speak. Nothing could be traced to them. They had forsaken him here, in some out of the way hole, so bound that he could not help himself, beyond the help of others, to a lingering death, such as the most exquisite enmity might deliberately devise.

But was he past his own help? He twisted and wriggled like an eel. The bag was so large that it did not confine his movements. The bands about his arms had been too hurriedly secured to make them perfect in their hold. The jar of the fall, too, had loosened them a trifle. Giles pulled his wrists up and down, encouraged by every trace of progress, till, after a long, long time, he triumphantly jerked one hand through the loop. It was a simple thing to cut the sacking away with his knife from about his head, and to free his ankles. He sat up, gazing inquisitively around him.

He lay down again on his stony bed, and laughed, — laughed till the hollow rocks resounded with his merriment. They had thrown him into the very pit from which he had clambered not twenty-four hours ago.

"What I have done once, I can assuredly do again," thought he.

He did not wear a sash to-day, and that he had left, hanging to the tree, was gone.

The rope that had been wound about him, and about the bag, would do as well. He made a sling of a bit of the sacking, tying one end of the cord to another, and a stone into the sling. It was a neat piece of work, not to be hurried. The sun was still high, and Giles wrought cheerfully at his task. The tree was not so hard to reach now, when he was less nervous, and surer that he should succeed. After a half-dozen futile efforts, the sling flew around its trunk. It fell into the pit, and he gathered it into his grasp, with the other end of the rope. He was badly cut in many places by his fall. He paid no heed to his injuries. Up the rope he went like a monkey. Once more he stood on the brink of the hole, looking about him. Afar in the distance, the only house in sight, the one landmark, was the highwayman's hut. He was loth to visit it, yet he knew no other refuge.

It was growing dusk when he reached the place. A piteous whinny came from a tumble-down shed in the rear of the larger building.

"They carried away the man," Giles exclaimed, "and forgot to take his horse. The very thing for me! Archie and George have mine; this is fair exchange for it, if I capture what should be George's — as his brother's heir. I will send it back to him when I reach home. How surprised he will be to receive it with my message."

He let the poor beast out of the stable after giving it water and food. He brought forth the saddle he found in the house and harnessed the animal, evidently a fine one, used to travel.

"We shall go far to-night," he said, stroking the horse's sleek sides. "Wilt thou carry me to my mother, and to little Meg?"

He was beginning to suffer from his long fast, but he could touch nothing from John Earl's house. He wheeled the impatient steed about, looked for some sign of the road, and then he thought: —

"I will leave it to the horse. He can lead me, for he knows his master's haunts. He shall take me where he will."

Giles's fixed determination was to seek his home at once. He would not run the chances of another encounter with the jester. He was confident that his guardian would guess the cause of his absence and soften any displeasure of the king's. He could send word to Sir Robert from Richmond. Meanwhile he had some money in his belt, — enough to keep himself and the horse.

Faithfully did the highwayman's thoroughbred justify his rider's trust. They speedily struck into such rough tracks as were reckoned then a tolerable sort of road. Mile by mile they went at a steady, rapid pace, and did not draw rein until Bedford was reached that night. Here they remained until an early hour of the morning. Then, refreshed and eager, they took the road again. On and on, to stop for food, or to give the noble beast the rest he never craved. The time went in an unvarying succession of such brief pauses, and of hard riding through St. Alban's, Watford, and Brentford, till Richmond came in sight.

Giles's eyes grew moist as he guided his horse into the well-known lane. Here was the copse where he found a bird's-nest full of twittering young ones once. Here was the blackberry tangle where he had gathered the fruit last summer with Jan and his pretty sister Annemie, and with little Meg in her scarlet cloak. Here was the home-field; there were the cows grazing beside the river. He stood in his stirrups and gave a lusty halloo. It was more than a month since he had left home; its chimneys were just rising above the woods.

As if his shout had called him, a boy's figure came into sight at the moment from behind the hedgerow. Giles gave another cry, for it was Jan.

"Is it really Giles?" exclaimed the page in French. "My dear friend, where do you come from?"

He gripped the other by the hand.

"Welcome!" he said, "thrice welcome. I never was so glad to see you. And, Giles," — he drew closer still to the horse's side, placing one hand on the pommel; he hesitated for a second, — "have you heard gossip of anything wrong?" he asked.

CHAPTER VI

IN THE OAK ROOM

Giles's brown cheek grew white. "My mother?" he gasped.

"No, no! Nothing is wrong with Madame Valentine; nor with your sister. This is a public matter that I would speak of."

Giles remembered the king's words to him, in the hall at Huntingdon, of those who come in contact with public affairs. It was strange, he thought, how he, until a few weeks ago, a home-abiding, quietly living boy, had been dragged of late into the doings of the English nation.

He flung himself from his horse, drawing one arm through the bridle.

"We can walk together towards the house," he said; "on the way you can tell me your meaning. First of all, though, Jan, how came you here?"

"That is soon explained. When her gracious Majesty died, your good mother sent for me. She said that I must wait at the Grange for word from my uncle in France as to what is to become of me. Nothing has been heard as yet, so I linger on here. I am content, you may suppose, with my pleasant life; yet I wish I knew what I am to do later on. Madame Valentine is kindness itself, now as always, to the son of her husband's old friend and comrade-in-arms."

"Yes, she loves you now for yourself. Before your uncle brought you here, she was desirous of seeing the face of Wilhelm Verrooy's only son, — he who, it chanced, was the one to hear my father's last messages before he died in those far Netherlands."

Giles's voice broke at the remembrance of the dark days when that sad intelligence was received at the Grange. Jan caught hold of his arm in a sympathizing pressure. "And now to what you had to tell me," the young Englishman went on.

Jan wrinkled his forehead in doubt. "I don't know how to put it. Any words may seem in excess of the facts. But, Giles, I am beginning to fear that all is not right with Master Wentworth."

"My tutor?"

"Yes. You remember how silent and reserved he is? I suspect something more now than silence and reserve behind that long visage of his. I believe him to be involved in a plot against the king."

"A plot against his Majesty? Oh, surely not already!"

"Hush! speak lower. The hedgerows may have ears. Yes, that there is a plot on foot I am confident. It may be that he is innocent in the matter; but he is altogether too friendly with one William Watson, who, I vow, is deep in some such scheme."

"Such scheme as what?"

"Of course I know nothing certainly. I mistrust it to be a plan to kidnap his Majesty. Watson visits your tutor often, and they hold secret conferences by the hour. Mine is the oak room, you know, next to Master Wentworth's. There are deep wardrobes between the two. Of late I have played the spy. Though I have only suspicion so far, I have built up a theory on broken sentences these two have let fall for me to overhear."

Giles looked, as he felt, deeply perplexed. "Is nothing clear enough to go upon?"

"No; there's the trouble. We cannot accuse any man, let alone a member of your household, on what I have so far heard. Giles, we must hear more!"

"I loathe this eavesdropping!" broke impatiently from the other.

Jan drew himself up haughtily. "Do you think it is congenial employment for me? Still I would lower myself farther than that to save your mother from the scandal that would arise if it were found some day that conspirators, in even the most abortive of plots, had been harbored underneath her roof."

"Yes, yes!" said Giles hastily. "Forgive me, Jan; I meant nothing against your honor. We could not afford to lose any chance to discover what might harm the king, or yet be hurtful to this home of mine. We must watch Master Wentworth; I see that clearly."

He shuddered at the recollection of what the consequences might be — not to James, for he had small opinion of his tutor's schemes, but to his gentle mother — should anything come to Archie's knowledge that could be turned against the Valentine household.

They were drawing near to the house. A tall, slender lady, in her black hood and veil, was strolling up and down across the bowling green. A little maiden played beside her, tossing her chestnut curls back, the better to see whom Jan was conducting to them. She gave another look from her bright dark eyes. She uttered a scream of pleasure.

"O mother, mother, look!" she called. "'T is Giles, our Giles!"

She was across the drawbridge and racing through the park like a whirlwind. Giles had never known so happy a moment as that in which he was clasped once more in those dear arms, and felt his sister clinging to his hand. A stifling sob rose in his throat. He remembered all Jan had hinted. He resolved: "I would stoop — yes, to the level of a spy — to save these two from harm!"

Master Wentworth appeared after they were seated at the supper ordered for the traveler. He said little, — he never said much, — but Giles was on his guard, and noticed how attentively he listened to every tiniest piece of information which was given in reply to Meg's countless questions relative to the king. The boy was careful in what he answered. It was natural that all of his small audience should wish to hear the details of his career at court. After they had separated for the night, Jan came to his room to say that he would keep up his watch.

"And if I hear what makes me sure of mischief, I shall come to you. Then you can listen yourself or not. I shall throw the responsibility into your hands."

Time went on. They heard of the king at Theobald's, where Cecil entertained him magnificently, and where he arranged his new privy council. Sixty-two titles of nobility were conferred. Wentworth told, without other comment than a sly smile, of a paper found fastened to the door of St. Paul's, offering lessons in the titles of the new nobles.

Then came word of the festivities at Stamford Hill. Here the royal train was met by the mayor and aldermen. A stag hunt, enjoyed by his Majesty above all things, had been so arranged that he should be conducted by it to the Charterhouse. From thence he proceeded to the Tower and Whitehall. His wife and two children — "Baby Charles" being too sickly to stand the journey — were twenty days behind him upon the road. He sent clothes and jewels from Elizabeth's collection to Berwick for the new queen, who was entertained at many country-houses along her route; at Althorpe, by a masque written by Ben Jonson. Finally news was received of the arrival at Windsor of her Majesty, Prince Henry, and her daughter Elizabeth.

One morning Giles and Jan went to court to see the reception of the Baron of Rosny, — afterwards famous in French history as Sully, — who came from Henry of Navarre. Little Meg was vastly entertained with their account of the gifts he brought: a superbly caparisoned horse for the king, a Venetian mirror set in gold and diamonds to the queen, and for Prince Henry a gold lance and a jeweled helmet. Though he had said nothing in advance of his intention, it turned out that Master Wentworth was also present on this occasion. He related a speech which some one had overheard a Scotch courtier make respecting the new ruler of England.

"Did ye ever see a jackanapes, mon? If so, ye must ken that if ye hauld him in your hand ye can gar him bite me; but if I hauld him, I can gar him bite ye."

This had been uttered in relation to the forthcoming treaty with France. Giles, however, applied it to himself and Archie, questioning whether the jester might not soon have his opportunity.

Two days later, when they went up the broad stairway together, Jan drew his friend in the direction of his own room.

"Come watch with me to-night," he said;

"I saw Watson enter the house as we came out from supper. I believe there will be mischief brewed before he leaves it."

"If we must, we must," Giles answered reluctantly. "I dare scarcely tread. If they hear me with you, they may guess our plans and be too sly for us."

Jan gave a little, noiseless laugh. "The tutor has no fear of me alone. He thinks I cannot understand English, because French is what I speak. I so soon found that it was wise to have that advantage of him, that I have never enlightened the good sir. Enter on tiptoe. Stand motionless until I make all secure and bid you stir again."

He bolted the door and moved rather noisily around the room, dragging a heavy chest forward, letting the fire-irons fall, and, under cover of this, motioning to Giles to steal forward to the dividing wall and slide behind the tapestry into a wardrobe's recess.

Jan removed his riding-boots with another thump upon the floor. With lightest step he crept across the Turkey rug to a position beside his friend. They pressed closely against the crevice Jan's quick eyes had detected. The murmur of conversation came from the next room.

"What says Sir Griffin Markham?" inquired Wentworth.

"He is ready for the kidnaping. He thinks the times propitious. This intelligence, methinks, will deter even his foolhardiness."

"You call him foolhardy?"

"He would risk all. There were rumors that the guard of armed gentlemen that slept at Greenwich had been increased, yet he took no steps to find the truth of the tale. Ay, I call him foolhardy, man."

The boys had by no means caught every word of this talk. The last sentence or two came louder, in Watson's excitement.

"What is to be done?" Master Wentworth asked.

"I have seen Lord Grey to-day, and put the same question to him. He says that we must postpone the attempt till later, when our Scotch king goes to hunt at Hanworth."

Some further talk took place, but nothing more was disclosed. All appeared to relate to the story which had been already told. The two listeners, stiffened with their strained posture, crept out into the room.

"Come with me," Giles whispered. "Together we can discuss what shall be done."

They stole to the door, slid back the bolt,

and glided softly along the passage to the safer precincts of Giles's own quarters. Once here, they stood and faced each other, an exclamation of horror passing from one to another.

"Your guardian!" Jan began.

"How can I tell him?" Giles interrupted "It might entangle him — for he has a cunning enemy at court — in the affairs of this house. We must get rid of Master Wentworth without delay. Yet I cannot denounce him, Jan."

"Nor I. Heartily though I dislike the man, shocked as I am to hear this of him, I could not bring him to the block."

"My Lord Grey is a person of influence," Giles said doubtfully, at length. "How would it do to send him tidings instantly that the plot is known? I hate an anonymous letter, no less than the deed we have been forced into this night. But it may pull us out of our present difficulty. They could not act without Wilton, and he would tell the rest when he received the warning."

Jan thought well, on the whole, of this proposal. There was no sleep for the friends that night. They spent the long hours in concocting the sentences necessary in telling enough, yet not too much, — in so disguising the script as to conceal its authorship, and possibly to thus enhance the authority of its words.

In the early light, Giles disappeared from the house. His colleague was to explain his absence without arousing suspicion. When he reappeared, the family were assembled on the green, watching the feats of horsemanship with which Jan was amusing Meg.

There were exclamations and inquiries. In the midst of them, Giles stole a look at his friend which was received and understood. The warning had been given.

Preparations were making for the coronation. In spite of the plague, which was raging in London, the Valentine household looked forward to viewing what the public might see of this august event. About three weeks beforehand, one morning, Giles entered the library for his usual Latin reading. His tutor was striding up and down the room, wringing his hands and sobbing like a child. Tears streamed down his stern, set face.

"What is wrong?" asked the boy, eyeing him in amazement.

"All is lost!" Wentworth cried.

"What do you mean?"

Giles's sharp tone was intended to recall him to himself. He passed one hand confusedly across his forehead. "I have had dire intelligence," said he.

"Of what?"

"It seems, although it was none of my devising, there has been a plot hatched to carry off his Majesty. He was to be kept in confinement till he made certain concessions. If he refused, the Lady Arabella Stuart was to be raised to the throne. I swear I knew naught of the rogues' doings, yet some of them were my best friends. The foul thing was planned for the Hanworth hunt, last month. Lord Grey postponed it then, and now Watson — thou hast seen Watson here? — has told the whole to one priest Gerard. He must needs carry it to Cecil. Right and left, men have been apprehended and thrown into prison" —

"Watson, too?" Giles inquired.

"Watson, too. But I am innocent, lad! Thou knowest that I am innocent?"

Giles's only answer to this assertion was a hint that it might be as well, in any case, to betray less agitation, and no sympathy with the conspirators. Master Wentworth thanked him almost servilely for the suggestion.

Jan opened the door and interrupted them.

"I have come for my task," said he. "Giles, you must ask our good master to excuse you. You have a visitor."

"A visitor?"

"Yes. It is a young sir from court. He gave his name as George Earl."

CHAPTER VII

FROM THE TOWER TO WINCHESTER

George Earl came forward very jauntily to meet his young host. He had been standing in the deep bay of the wainscoted morning-room. The sneer with which he had looked out upon the moat and the meadow still lingered on his lips. Giles thought he was gloating over the destruction of this happy home.

He bowed gravely to the intruder, not extending his hand.

"Art surprised to see me here?" inquired his guest. "I am come to thank thee for the safe return of my — of my horse." A quiver of pain, at the recollection of whose steed it had been, crossed his thin face. Giles was sorry, for the moment, for him.

"Perhaps I should apologize," he said coolly, making no motion towards a seat for himself, nor for young Earl, "for borrowing that gallant beast. I could not crave thy permission when we parted upon the moor."

George grew red. "I fail to understand" — he began.

"No matter. Hast other errand, may I inquire?"

A sly glance crept into the ferret eyes. "Thou seemst almost to expect it. Ay, have I. I come with tidings to thy good friend — what name hath he? Oh, Wentworth, Ralph Wentworth, I trow. Mayhap thou wilt break to him that his colleague, William Watson, hath been taken to the Tower."

Giles raised his eyebrows. "Tidings have but now reached us of the conspiracy, and of the arrest. Why thy solicitude for Master Wentworth?"

George could not admit his real motive, — that he came here in hopes to detect something amiss to carry with him back to court, now that the air was rife with surmises. "I thought to warn thee," he answered boldly, "that thy name hath been mentioned more than once this day in connection with thy tutor, and his friends, who have conceived this scheme of kidnaping his Majesty."

"Thou hast not as yet explained thy interest in me and my instructor," Giles replied; "nor how the fact that he was known to William Watson should bring him into the affair. But, if thy conscience is discharged of its duty, I shall be so inhospitable as to bid thee good-morrow, Master Earl."

He bowed low in mock courtesy. George's eyes glittered dangerously. "Not so fast," he said. "I have some queries to put to thee. Thine own share in this plot; it may be" —

A door opened behind them.

"Giles," said a gentle voice, "thy guest, — will he not break his fast with us?"

The boys turned in the direction of the sound. Mistress Valentine stood on the threshold, her sweet, pale face framed in the time-stained oak. She extended one hand frankly.

"I am rejoiced to meet, under my roof, any friend of my son's," she said.

Giles felt as if he must step between George Earl and that dear figure, innocent of harm, knowing nothing of what this new-comer had done in the past, nor what was his errand now. Even George's malignity was not proof against the lady's serene unconsciousness. He sank on one knee, kissed her fingers, and then, muttering some excuse, he hurried from the room.

Giles brushed unceremoniously past his mother, fixed in her surprise at this curious conduct, and followed George to the hall. He would not betray anything like cowardice. George stood still for an instant to say: —

"I could not break her bread. No! Nor would I harm her, when she spoke thus to me! But thou" —

A glare of hatred was sufficient finish to the sentence.

Giles bowed low once more. "We shall meet again," he said. And neither boy guessed when nor how that meeting should come to pass.

All sorts of rumors flew about, in those next few weeks before St. James's Day, when the coronation took place. Watson, with his accomplices, made many so-called confessions. None, happily, implicated Master Wentworth, who was recommended to take a journey to his home in Yorkshire, and thus was put out of the way for a time. After all, he was too small game. The conspirators accused Lord Cobham and Sir Walter Raleigh. The excitement was feverish when these two were committed to the Tower. The tale ran that Lord Grey's had been but a bye-plot (the name under which it has come down in history) to a main plot that concerned Cobham and Raleigh.

The plague spread. King James went to the palace, but would not proceed thence to the Tower, for the procession to Westminster. This was one grievous disappointment to the throngs of people. Another was that St. James's fair was forbidden to be held in the precincts of the palace. Every precaution was taken against the double terrors of plague and plot.

The royal couple went to Westminster by water. Meg, clinging to her brother's hand, was impressed with the appearance of her Majesty, whose lovely hair hung upon her shoulders, while she wore a golden crown. Directly after the ceremony the court repaired to Woodstock, to be out of the way of contagion. It was a dull, dreary summer, with constant apprehension from illness, or from some new story of a stratagem against King James. Jan's uncle sent word from France that, till the plague should abate, he could not risk a visit to England, and he plainly did not wish his nephew to resort to him while there was any like chance of bringing the disease.

With the autumn came the trial of the plotters, and that remarkable defense which Raleigh made for himself. It was currently reported, during the summer, that he had attempted suicide in his despair. The two boys made their way into the trial chamber to hear Sir Walter, for whom they entertained much sympathy, since scarcely any one shared the court's impression of his guilt. They were present at the tragic scene when Elizabeth's old courtier was convicted of high treason.

Watson was executed not long after this. To Giles's horror one day, in visiting his guardian at Winchester, where the court was now removed, he spied the head of his tutor's old friend and accomplice set up on the castle tower.

A wet November morning brought the time when Lord Grey, Sir Griffin Markham, and Lord Cobham were to be beheaded. The boys went with all the masculine world of London to witness this last passage of the Bye. The sheriff first brought out Sir Griffin, looking very serious, but with a firm and haughty step. A handkerchief was handed to him. He pushed it aside.

"I can face death without blushing," said he.

A hand was laid on Giles's arm. A panting, hurrying figure pushed between Jan and himself. A man, whose dress had been torn by the crowd, whose face was white and strained, raised himself upon the boys' shoulders.

"Lift me up!" he muttered hoarsely. "Lift me up! 'Tis a matter of life and death!"

The friends complied. Holding the stranger above the heads of the throng, they saw that he waved a paper frantically towards the sheriff.

"A message," he called, — "a message from his Majesty!"

Sir Benjamin Tichborne motioned the man — it was King James's clerk — to a private conference. By and by he came back to Sir Griffin, who had stood quietly in his place.

"As you are so ill-prepared," he said, "you shall have two hours' grace."

Markham looked astonished, but merely bowed. He was led from the scaffold, and locked into the castle hall.

Lord Grey was brought forth. He was foppishly dressed, surrounded by a group of young men friends. He knelt, and began a prayer for himself, and, when that was finished, one for the king. This lasted for an hour, during which the crowd stood silent in the rain. When the condemned man rose to his feet, Sir Benjamin stepped forward.

"The order has been changed," he announced; "Lord Cobham is to precede you, sir," and led the bewildered man back to where Markham was waiting in the castle.

Lord Cobham was now brought to the scaffold. He began a speech in which he persisted in the story he had told against Raleigh,— a story the latter declared to be the silliest of falsehoods. A moment of silence fell. All watched what the sheriff would do. All were thunderstruck to see Lord Grey and Sir Griffin once more led forth and together. The three men stared at each other in bewilderment.

"Gentlemen," said Sir Benjamin, "his Majesty, in his mercy, has vouchsafed your lives to you."

A mighty shout went up,— a shout that rose to the heavens. Giles pointed to a window of the tower, and a face that looked down on them. "See, Jan!" he said; "Sir Walter Raleigh listens. Let us pray that it is a token of good for him."

The next morning brought a note to Giles from Carey, bidding him go to Winchester on some errand for himself. The writer was at his home near by, but did not wish his ward to visit him.

"I am not well," he added, " and, though I have none of the fear of the great sickness that is felt at court, nor any thought that my megrims may prove the like, yet, 't is wise to take precautions. Thus I have shut myself up here for a season."

The business at the castle did not warrant delay. Thither Giles proceeded at once. He was graciously received by the member of the Privy Council whom Sir Robert had told him to seek out. A singular apparition joined Bruce as Giles was making his farewell. It was a Frenchman, clad in jewel-trimmed velvet clothes of priceless value. He wore gloves of finest leather that exhaled an overpowering perfume. Pearls were twined in his hair, and his cheeks were painted. A tiny lap-dog peeped from one pocket of his coat. The boy did not know that he looked upon one of the last of the Mignonnes of Henry Third of France.

He was quitting the royal household, as unobtrusively as might be, when he was hailed by an imperious yet pleasant salutation. A youth of his own age hurried after him, catching him by the hand.

"Thou 'rt Giles Valentine, art thou not?" he asked.

It was Prince Henry, the heir to the throne.

Giles dropped to his knees. With right good-will he kissed the hand of the best and the most brilliant of all the Stuart line. The handsome, gay little fellow snatched away his fingers, and gave him a playful tap.

"Tut, tut!" he cried. "No homage! What are we save two young rogues together? And thou hast won thy spurs. I have long wished to see the lad who took that famous ride into Scotland. Bruce told me of thy visit, just in time to overtake thee. Come!" He linked his arm through Giles's. "Thou art my prisoner."

They both laughed. Giles thought, if this boy were king, how willingly he would lay down his life for Henry the Ninth. But Henry the Ninth was never to reign.

"Thou knowest George Earl?" the prince rattled on. "Ah! so I have been told" (with a shrewd glance at his companion). "Didst hear that he was ill, lying in yon outhouse?" Giles uttered an exclamation. "Oh, naught serious," said Henry lightly. "Or so Archie told us, and Archie has full charge of him."

"But these illnesses,"— Giles began uneasily.

"I tell thee this is naught. Stay, we will stop at the door and inquire. I like thee, good Giles, for thine anxiety."

"My prince, you must not go."

"Wilt not believe me when I say 't is naught? Ah, here is Archie. He will allay thy fears. Nay? Why, Archie, man, what is it?"

The fool burst from the building towards which their steps were bent. He flew past them, huddled into a heap of terror, not noting Giles, but, even in his passion of fear, with the sense to make a wide circuit from the royal boy. His face was buried in a handkerchief.

"Back, back!" he shrieked. "'T is the plague! The swelling has come 'neath his arm. 'T is the plague. I tell you, keep away!"

Henry was every inch the prince as he thundered out:—

"And who is with the lad?"

"No one,— no one. Who would bide with the stricken? Your highness, I tell you, away!"

And with that Archie was gone.

Henry made one bound towards the entrance. Quick as he was, Giles was before him. He seized his sovereign's son about the waist.

"Are you mad?" he hissed between his teeth. "You shall not enter there."

"And leave the dying alone? For shame! Unhand me, ere I strike."

"Strike, an it pleaseth you. Nay, of what avail? I am the stronger. You shall not go. I will take care of Earl. I will shut myself inside that room. But cross the threshold you shall not!"

"He is our servant," Henry gasped, "and our charge. 'T is no concern of thine, for he is not thy friend."

"Ay, it is my concern, for he is mine enemy."

They reached the spot in their wrestling struggle. The prince drew himself together for a final effort. Giles was on the alert. He loosened the other's grasp by one sudden movement. He made a dash and threw his weight against the door. It fell in with him. He was inside, and he slid the bolt.

CHAPTER VIII

ENTER GUY FAWKES

"My kind nurse," murmured George feebly, "lay thee down and take thy rest."

"Thou art mending," Giles answered, stooping over the pallet where the invalid was stretched. He set down his dish of cooling drink, and took the skeleton fingers in his. "Thy fever is abated; thy pulse beats stronger. Please God, we shall bring thee out of this." He smiled down upon George who, to his grief, burst into a flood of childish tears.

"Under Providence, 't is all thy doing," he answered, while Giles strove in vain to soothe him. "Thou hast watched beside me night and day. Thou hast given me fondest care. Thou hast gone without food or sleep, lest I suffer. And I — what have I done to thee?"

"Hush, lad. Thou shalt not agitate thyself like this. By and by. Wait till thou art stronger, if thou wouldst bring up the past."

"No, I cannot," he sobbed. "'T is not out of my mind for a moment. I dwell on naught save thy kindness and my base conduct. Giles, 't was I that stole thy gold and thy medal."

"Ay, George," his nurse answered, patting his hand; "I guessed as much."

"Is 't so? And — and I was one to waylay thee, and cast thee in the pit, like Joseph's wicked brethren."

"But I escaped, like Joseph," said Giles with a smile. "Why tell me this, poor lad?"

"'T is a relief. And one thing more. I have tried to injure thee to his Majesty. There was not much that I could do. Yet what influence was mine was given against thee. And — there was another more powerful adversary, working ever to poison the king's mind, Giles."

The listener understood that he did not wish to mention Archie by name, although it was plain that the confession was a warning for him to beware of the jester's schemes.

"I am such a harmless subject," he rejoined, to reassure his informant. "How could my sovereign be made to believe that a mere boy threatened his throne?"

"Boy or man, none is to be despised in these times. I tell thee to be on thy guard against the effects of what has already been done. Naught more will be essayed against thee; at the least I can promise that."

It was certainly probable that the fool, although he still kept aloof from his nephew's sick-room, himself would be grateful to Giles, who had proved the stancher friend. Through Prince Henry, those in quarantine had been supplied with food and drink and medical attendance. Archie, too, sent messages by the physician.

"Thou wilt forgive me, Giles?" pleaded George.

"I forgive thee freely. Now bide still and sleep."

"If thou wouldst rest!"

"I will," Giles answered with an inspiration. "If thou wilt lie quite quietly, I will throw myself down beside thee and mayhap I too may sleep."

George eagerly assured him that he would not stir. Giles intended only to compose the other, forcing him to the repose his weak state demanded. He, too, was utterly worn out. After a short time of listening to his patient's regular breath, of watching beneath his half-closed eyelids the peaceful slumber into which the invalid sank, he lost consciousness and knew no more.

He was aroused by a subdued, impatient rapping upon the door. He staggered to his feet, rubbing his heavy eyes.

"Who knocks?" he asked, stealing across the room.

"'T is I, — Carey. Giles, I must have speech with thee."

Instantly the boy knew that something was wrong at home. His hand faltered that would fain unbolt the door which stood between himself and liberty. His sense of duty kept him where he stood.

"I cannot open," he said. "'T is a plague-stricken spot."

"Lad, this is no time for parley," was the response. "And I have but just arisen from the plague."

Giles gave a cry of surprise. His scruples vanished; he threw open the door and stepped outside. His guardian grasped his hand.

"My good, brave boy," he exclaimed. "Would that the tidings I brought thee were less heavy!"

"My mother?"

"Thy mother is ill, Giles." It was the

court physician who spoke. He stood beside Sir Robert. "We have deemed it right to send thee to her."

Giles looked up piteously into his face. "But the chance of contagion?" he said.

"My dear lad, there is no danger."

He understood that his mother was struck down with the plague.

He clasped his hands in desperation. "How can I leave George?" he asked.

"I will attend to that. Trust me, he shall not suffer. Nay, go now while he sleeps. 'T is the better way. And, mayhap, 't were well that thou shouldst hasten."

Giles lost hope from that moment. His guardian had a horse waiting for him. Their ride was so conducted that they held no intercourse with others upon the road. Sir Robert had brought fresh clothing for his charge, who left that which was tainted with infection to be burned by the surgeon. They had also food in their saddle-bags, and they made rare halts for rest until the chimneys of the Grange came once more into sight.

What was known of the lady's seizure was imparted to her son as they rode. It was the result of her charity. She had heard through her servants that Sir Robert lay neglected in a home whence all the other members had fled at the first symptoms of his disease. She had gone to him, accompanied by the physician who attended the two families. She had saved his life, the grateful man declared; Giles saw that he feared it might be at the expense of her own.

Indeed, there was not one sign in her favor. She recognized her children, and welcomed her only son. She commended him for what he had done at Winchester, telling him how entirely Jan had tried to take his place at her side. She gave little Meg into her brother's care. Evidently their future weighed heavily upon her mind. Mistress Valentine had a last wish to express to Giles's guardian. It was that he and his sister might be surrendered to Jan's French uncle when he should come for Jan.

"His wife will look after my little girl," she said, almost at the very last. "Meg will need a woman's influence. And she will have a companion in Annemie Verrooy."

Giles reached his home on Christmas Eve. The Christmas sun rose brightly on the desolate house. It found these children motherless.

Perhaps it was well for the boy — Meg was

too young to comprehend the extent of her loss — that he sickened, after all need for further exertion was over, and lay for weeks in a prostrate condition, even when his most alarming symptoms were passed. Jan and the little girl escaped, but Dame Tryon, Mistress Valentine's attendant, and her children's old nurse, fell ill, requiring long-continued care. So the winter wore slowly away. With the spring, since M. Chapelain did not appear from Paris, while Sir Robert's duties at court kept him constantly away from home, he rented the Grange to old acquaintances of the family. The understanding was that Meg was to be looked after here for the present, while the boys went to a tutor in London.

This arrangement would have been admirable if the preceptor had proved trustworthy. Master Carr soon showed himself careless of his charges, while absorbed in his own affairs. He was a profound scholar, engaged upon a book of disputation. As soon as the day's lessons were finished he shut himself into his study, not emerging to know anything of the youths' employment.

They spent many idle hours wandering about the ugly, straggling suburbs of the town. Often night found them at a distance from home. They had money at their command, and no account to render to Master Carr; so they rather enjoyed a search for lodgings.

"Where are we now, Giles?" the young Dutchman asked.

They had gone on a long tramp into the country. Giles, who usually acted as leader, had proposed their stopping at Saint Clement's Inn for the night. Dusk was falling, but no sign of hostelry appeared. Giles was looking about him irresolutely when his friend put the question.

"I have no idea. We must have missed the road. I see no house. Wait! what is that there in the midst of the fields?"

"It is a house," said Jan. "But surely it is not Saint Clement's."

"No matter. The inmates cannot refuse us entrance. We can pay them well. It looks like a poor place where gold might open the door if pity would not."

"There is no light whatever," Jan observed after they had stumbled forward to a nearer view. "The house is empty."

"All the better. This is an adventure indeed. If the door is bolted it will be hard if we cannot raise a window."

This proved necessary. They tried several entrances, finally coming on a loose sash which could be pried up from the outside. Jan was a slender, lithe little fellow. He pushed himself, though not without some difficulty, through the narrow aperture. He opened the door, let his friend in, and they made all secure again. Their refuge was a mere hovel,— a room below, and two apparently above this, one reached by a stairway, the other by a rough ladder. It was a boyish freak that induced them to climb to this last chamber and pull the ladder up after them.

They made themselves a bed upon the floor.

"Hark!" Jan whispered.

"It is the wind."

"No, it is not the wind. Hark!"

There were steps in the room beneath them. The outer door had opened. Through chinks in the floor they saw a lantern glimmer, and then that it was shut off. All was darkness, yet their eyes, now accustomed to the gloom, could make out a circle of shadowy forms. It was characteristic of the dreadful state of the kingdom, and of what the last year had brought forth, that neither had a single thought now of the meanness of eavesdropping: all they had in mind was that some terrible iniquity was brewing, and it was their duty to discover it.

The door opened again very softly and two more men entered. Murmured greetings followed. Some one went to the windows and hung a cloak at each one. The lantern slide flew back. The watchers saw a group of five dark-faced men, all gloomy determination and savage daring. One after another they sank upon their knees. Each one, as his name was called, took an awful oath of secrecy. They were Robert Catesby, Thomas Winter, Guy Fawkes, Thomas Percy, and John Wright.

They clustered close about the one who called himself Catesby.

"This is my plan," said he. "Speak ye if a better could be devised. Vinegar House at Westminster is to be let. It has a shed against the House of Parliament. Through it a hole may be cut in the foundation wall and powder introduced" —

There was an outcry. The boys, for a wild moment, thought that it came from themselves. But it was John Wright who had uttered the word "Shame!"

"Shame?" repeated Catesby, turning on him. "Have we no right to use such measures as come to hand with the Scottish swine, who take away our property, our gold, our liberty of conscience? Any weapon against them, say I."

"But this would mean the Commons as well; the bishops " —

"Ay, and the king, and the Prince of Wales. We shall wipe them all out of existence. Come, man, be wise. Reflect that, if we strike, we must strike hard."

John Wright heaved a deep sigh. It was echoed by Winter. The other three looked scornfully defiant.

"And now we will seek Garnet," said Catesby. "He lies in the chamber above. Methinks," as a gentle snore was heard, "he sleeps the sleep of a just man."

The boys seized each other madly. That sound came close to them. Could it be that there was another occupant of the garret, whose presence they had not suspected before? Were those desperate fellows about to enter their room and discover them?

No. They made their way to the staircase. They heard them steal up one by one. They caught the tones of some one roused from sound slumber on the other side of the thin partition wall. The murmur of conversation came to them. They dared not move to listen closer at hand.

By and by the men crept down the stairway again. They conferred together shortly. They unbolted the door. They had all quitted the house before the boys drew a long breath, or stirred from their fixed position.

CHAPTER IX

THE GUNPOWDER PLOT

"There is, at least, time for consideration," said Giles, as they left the dreadful house. They had waited for daylight, that they might not run across any watchers lurking outside.

"Yes. Their fiendish plot will require months of preparation." Jan assented. "And, happily, we know the very spot where they will be employed. We can keep an eye on them, while we are making up our minds what it is best to do. Do you suppose it would be wisest to take the whole thing at once, in such detail as we have collected, to your guardian at the court?"

"I doubt it," Giles replied. "Think, when the Bye was frustrated, how Raleigh was dragged into it. Sir Robert is known to have been disappointed by the position given him. His Majesty's mind has been colored by Archie's hints. No. Frankly, I dare not tell my guardian, for his own good. Not unless we resort to that in the end, in desperation."

Boys such as these, bright, constantly upon the watch, made the cunningest of spies, where men, about the same business, would have been soon detected. They learned that one Thomas Percy had rented the Westminster House. Robert Kay, evidently a new member of the band, had taken another at Lambeth, whence fagots, coal, and powder were conveyed, little by little, by Fawkes, who was represented to the world as Percy's servant. Sir Robert innocently told the friends one day, in a visit to them, that Percy had obtained a license from King James to collect a troop in the service of the Archduke Albert in Flanders. Catesby, he said, was to be a captain in this enterprise, and both men were gathering together arms and horses.

Jan trod on Giles's foot underneath the table. This, of course, was part of the conspiracy; these were preparations for the one horrible event.

One day, Jan urged a reflection that had been harassing him of late. George Earl, they heard, had gone to Scotland to recruit his health. Archie was with the court. Although his insinuations against Giles might have ceased since his nephew's illness, what he had said in the past was probably remembered by the king, — not only against Carey, but also against his ward. Would it not all be revived if it ever came out that the boy had been acquainted with the workings of this gunpowder plot?

"I understand the hazards of my position," Giles answered steadily. "Well, I can only do my duty as it appears to me, leaving the result in the hands of Providence."

By hanging about Vinegar House, and seizing their opportunity, the boys managed to slip inside. They found a close, dark closet on the ground floor, from which they could hear a good deal and see something of what was going on. Their lives, they thoroughly appreciated, were in jeopardy. They were obliged to be careful beyond words to describe. For the plotters, now eight in number, had laid in a supply of food, and left the place so seldom that there was always some one on guard. Happily their work in the cellar was such close employment that Jan and Giles did get in and out of the upper floor unseen by them. They were trying to undermine the foundation, but water ran in on them, making this impossible. Then they began to bore through the wall. It was labor to which none of them was accustomed. There were many mishaps when the stones were moved: they had been laid three yards thick, and the task was endless.

The crash of one of these rocks, as it fell one morning to the ground, was followed by a strange noise overhead. Again Giles caught his companion in a nervous grasp; again, as in the house by St. Clement's Inn, he supposed the sound came from close to themselves, and that detection was inevitable. Jan was beset by another alarm. He believed the foundations of the building had been shaken; that it was falling about their heads.

They heard the rapid running of feet up the cellar steps. They held their breath. They did not move as the man came nearer their hiding-place. He passed them, and went on out of doors. After a long interval he returned. They could tell by his descending footfalls that he was reëntering the cellar.

"'T is a coal dealer," said Guy Fawkes, "removing his stock from vaults beneath the Parliament House. He goes into business elsewhere."

Percy dropped his pickaxe. "The very

thing!" he exclaimed. "Guy, thou shalt hire it in my name, an the place be to let. Thither thou canst convey the powder and the fagots. Friends, it is given into our hands. We need not thus to strive to enter it from without."

The boys gathered further that, since spring was advancing, nothing was to be done, beyond such plans as these for the storing of the powder, until Parliament should assemble in the autumn. There was no more for them to discover here, after they had seen thirty-six barrels, whose deadly contents they could guess, carried into the vaults next door, with armfuls of wood and wagon-loads of coal. Now Jan devised an idea, and, during the long days of summer, they were prepared to carry it into effect.

They had overheard the names of several new conspirators who had recently joined the party. One was a John Grant, living near Stratford, an acquaintance of Wentworth, who, they were told, was staying with him. Under cover of a wish to see Giles's old tutor, they might seek out this man. Perhaps they could let fall a hint that, while it shielded themselves from any share in the scheme, should warn Grant that the plot was known.

This much they could do in safety. Obtaining permission from Master Carr to absent themselves, they set out for Warwickshire.

After various misadventures, they were set upon the way to the house they sought. It was a dark and gloomy spot, shut in by frowning walls, on the outskirts of the quiet village, and giving a glimpse of the river Avon. The boys inquired at the gate for Wentworth.

"He left Stratford this morning," the lodge-keeper answered, "to return to Yorkshire. If ye are fain to follow him, he has five hours' start."

They exchanged glances of dismay. "What is to be done now?" Jan asked, speaking, as usual, in French.

"At least we must see the master of the house," was the reply in the same language. "It may be that we can do something with him. But this absence of Master Wentworth is a severe blow to our device."

They were ushered into the presence of Grant, a nervous, frail-looking man. As Giles and his friend entered the room he was tearing up a letter. He stooped to collect the scraps of paper before he spoke to them, or motioned them to seats.

"Your errand, young sirs?" he said, in tones that betrayed agitation.

Giles bent forward to catch his shifty eye. "We came seeking my one-time tutor, Master Wentworth. Would you hear our mission to him?"

Grant sank uneasily into the depths of an immense oaken chair. "As you will," he answered coldly. The boys thought his white fingers twitched in their grasp upon the bits of paper.

"We meant to warn him," Giles went on, speaking steadily, though his heart beat fast, "that he had been on the brink of accusation in the Bye. It might not go as well with him another time, if he were found so close to a bigger plot when exposure came."

Grant jumped to his feet. His movement was so violent that the great chair was overthrown. "What meanst thou?" he stuttered. "The Parliament — the — the commissioners — have they discovered aught?"

"Mayhap you mean the commissioners for the union of England and Scotland," Jan interrupted coolly; "those who have been lodged at Vinegar House in Westminster. What should they have discovered?"

"I know not," the miserable wretch replied.

He spent a moment readjusting his chair in its place. "The mention of a plot — that was it. I fail to understand thee," looking at Giles, "with thy half sentences. What meanst thou, boy?"

Giles saw Jan stoop, as if to put a damask cushion in its place. He saw, too, without the apparent flicker of an eyelash, that his colleague had gathered a bit of paper, in that swift movement, into his palm.

"A word to the wise is proverbially sufficient," he answered courteously. "Sir, we intend but kindness, and no harm. We come from London. You here, safe hid away from the turmoil of that life, may not guess what talk there arises of stratagems and schemes. 'T was in these we meant to beg Master Wentworth to refrain from show of complicity. And now farewell."

Grant raised his hand in detention. "Meant you some special plot? Have ye heard aught of one?"

With perfect truth they could say, Yes. Indeed they had heard sufficient, from Catesby and his followers, to warrant a full assent. Of course Grant understood them to mean that the matter was known to the world. His pale face grew whiter.

"It hath not reached the court?" he asked.

"I think not yet," Giles answered. "You may well see that it is only a question of time. All will be speedily laid before the king."

Grant reached out a hand, which Giles pretended not to see.

"I thank ye both," he said, his voice shaking with terror. "I thank ye in Master Wentworth's name. I will devise means to let him know what ye say. And now you will have some refreshment?"

"Naught whatever, sir," they cried in a breath. "Time presseth," Jan went on. "We must be far on our road to-night."

They bowed and left the room. Giles glanced back, for a last look, and saw their host fallen sidewise in the oaken chair. His trembling fingers tapped his chin. His features were dark with thought.

No sooner were they outside the garden, and the lodge gate closed behind them, than Jan opened his tightly shut fingers. He held up the scrap they had concealed.

"See my prize!" he cried. "Let us read it together."

Giles looked over his shoulder.

"A cipher!" he exclaimed in sore disappointment.

"Not at all. What rare good fortune! You remember Fawkes said he had been in the Netherlands. 'T is Dutch, boy, and from Guy, I take it. It reads, —

"'Parliament has been prorogued from October to November. Can it be that we are mistrusted?'"

CHAPTER X

AT HOLBEACH

The boys felt much relieved as they galloped along the country roads on their way back to town.

"The plot has been discovered," Giles said excitedly, "without any appearance of you or me in the unveiling. The country is safe, and so are our necks!"

"I doubt," the more cautious Jan responded, "that all fear is past of our seeing the inside of the Tower. I do wish" (with a long-drawn breath) "that we were outside England."

"Where could we go? To your distracted Netherlands?" For Jan's uncle had been during the past summer in Holland, sent by the French government on affairs of state.

"Better there than here," Jan contended stoutly. "But, alas! it is little use wishing. They are the dark schemes of troubled London, into which we are throwing ourselves once more."

So they approached the city. Jan went straight to Westminster, while Giles sought out White Webbs, a lonely house near Enfield Chase, which they knew the conspirators had lately hired. In this manner, when they met later on at their lodgings, both had something to tell of what they had gathered from their perilous observation. Jan said that Fawkes was fully reassured. The commissioners had walked over the spot where his barrels of powder were concealed, and talked easily together the while. The postponement of Parliament might be due to several causes. He was confident that it was not from detection of the plot.

Giles had learned still more. There were recent accessions to the ranks. Sir Everett Digby had given a large sum of money. He was to invite his friends to a hunting party in Warwickshire, so that they should be gathered together in readiness to take up arms as soon as the train of powder had been fired. Fawkes was to use a slow-match, which would give him time to take a boat before the explosion, and reach a ship ready to convey him to Flanders.

The Princess Elizabeth was to be proclaimed Queen after the death of her father and brothers, if Charles was of the royal party; otherwise he was to reign. A wealthy country gentleman, Francis Tresham, was among the later plotters, and, Giles said, was felt by the others — he was Catesby's convert, and brought in because of his long purse — to be of so fickle a nature as to endanger the success of anything he undertook.

"Catesby himself regrets his presence, now it is too late," the boy added. "I heard him complain to several of the company of the dreadful dreams that were tormenting him. He is losing heart."

"Is the time set for the 5th?" asked Jan.

"Yes, but there is a hitch. Almost every plotter has some friend whom he wishes to save. Catesby, alone, stands out, utterly bloodthirsty. He says he would lose his own son rather than run any danger of revealing the plot by putting him upon his guard. The rest could not see it in the same light. It is agreed that each who chooses to do so shall send some message to a friend, bidding him stay away from the house that day. Those warnings give us our opportunity, Jan."

"Yes," Jan thoughtfully assented, "That is our chance. This fickle Tresham, — whom does he desire to save?"

"His brother-in-law, Lord Monteagle."

"Let us watch his brother-in-law. We can reach the council best through him, I fancy."

Lord Monteagle's movements were readily learned. On the night of October 27, the two heard that he had sent orders to his house at Hoxton to have supper for him. They were lurking outside when he arrived. Presently a tall, dark man, wrapped in a long cloak, appeared from the shadow of the wall. He had been on the lookout, too. The friends were sauntering easily along, arm in arm. There was nothing suspicious in their air. The man held out a letter to Giles.

"I will give thee a piece of gold," he began, "if thou wilt deliver this into the hands of my lord."

Giles did not move his fingers even to push away the coin. He could not so much as touch the thing that was cursed because of its owner. For he guessed this to be Francis Tresham.

"I will take your message," he answered.

"Give it to none else than my lord himself."

"It shall be done."

The man glided away. Giles demanded

entrance at the door, while Jan waited for him under the wall outside. There was the excuse of an important letter. Giles was admitted to Monteagle's presence. He surrendered the paper with the explanation that a passer-by in the street had urgently begged him to see it delivered. The master of the house tore open the sheet. He stared at its contents in blank surprise.

"A feigned hand," he muttered. "Neither signed nor dated. Here, Ward," handing it over to one of his esquires. "Read the whole aloud!"

Giles's memory always retained a few sentences of that letter, of which he thus heard the contents.

"'Out of the love I have to some of your friends, I have a care of your preservation. . . . I would advise you, as you tender your life, to devise some excuse to shift attendance at this Parliament. . . . I say they shall receive a terrible blow, this Parliament.'"

My lord sprang up. "I must to Whitehall ere I sleep!" said he.

Giles rejoined his companion outside the gate. "All is well!" he cried, flinging an arm about Jan's neck. "All is well, and we have not been seen to move in it at all."

Jan made no answer.

Sir Robert came a little later to look to their welfare before taking a journey to Ireland on the king's business. He spoke of rumors at court, of a gigantic plot against all the heads of the nation. Monteagle had brought a letter concerning it, to show to James.

"Our hands are washed of it all," said Giles, after his guardian had taken his leave.

"I hope they may be," Jan answered. "And, lad! since there is no further good purpose to serve, don't go near Westminster nor White Webbs again."

Giles opened his eyes very wide. "Are you grown timid?" he said in jest.

"Yes, and none too soon. Can you not see that we two have been too often hanging about those men? We have visited Grant, and you were Tresham's messenger to Lord Monteagle. It is high time to think of our own good."

"Ah, but I must see what Fawkes is about in the vaults," Giles pleaded. "Just one more visit, Jan, and I shall be prudence itself henceforth. Only let me witness the end of the tragedy."

Jan shook his head, but his friend had his

way. On Monday he went to Westminster, where he saw my Lord Chamberlain and Monteagle looking about the House of Lords, as if in preparation for the next day's reception of the king. They made an excuse about some missing hangings to go down into the vaults. Guy Fawkes stood in one corner beside a pile of fagots.

"What art doing here?" demanded Suffolk.

"I am Master Percy's servant, an't please my lord," he answered. "I am looking after my master's stock of fuel."

"Thy master has a good stock," said Monteagle. And so they left him.

Giles was too excited to quit the spot. He found himself an old hiding-place in a corner of the building. He watched there, through that long night, for what should happen. He saw a guard of soldiers gather, and knew that the end was near. Midnight was called by the watchman, and one o'clock, and two. A tall, cloaked figure crept up out of the vault. There was a murmured word of command. The soldiers moved forward like one body. Guy Fawkes was surrounded. The men bound him hand and foot, he making neither sound nor movement when he saw how useless resistance would be. The commander, a Westminster magistrate, descended into the vault. Giles pushed behind him in the mob. Back of the door was a dark lantern burning. The fagots were quickly pulled from their places. Hogsheads and barrels were found beneath them. The soldiers tapped one after another. From each trickled the same thin stream of a dark, odorous powder.

Sir Thomas Knevett came out of the cellar. He pointed towards his prisoner. "To his Majesty," he said. "He shall examine into this matter." And leaped upon his horse.

Giles knew that he should return home to Jan, who would be watching for him. He knew that he should keep himself out of any further implication with the discovery. But he was rash enough to go to White Webbs, instead, to see how the other plotters bore the arrest of Fawkes. The conduct of these men, for that last month before the complete disclosure, has always remained a mystery. Besides such warnings as Grant must have given them, Monteagle's letter was repeated to one of them, in substance, by Ward. Their boldness is hard to credit. Giles found that Percy and Winter were mounting to ride to Dunmoor. Keyes and Rookwood, he learned, were to wait until the following morning for the latest news.

When Giles fell into his bedroom, full of the story which Jan must awaken to hear, prudence flew to the winds. Both were tingling with the electricity with which all London was charged. At noon they found themselves, they could not have told how, waiting on horseback to witness the flight of the White Webbs party. They had not discussed it together, yet they understood that they intended to follow these men and see them brought to bay. Keyes had already quitted the house. Rookwood rode forth at noon. At Brickhill he overtook Catesby with John Wright. Soon afterwards they fell in with Percy and Christopher Wright. They rode at the top of their speed, outstripping the boys, who saw them fling their cloaks over a hedge to lighten their weight. When the home of Catesby's mother was reached, at Ashby, Saint Leger's, Rookwood had gone eighty miles in the six hours. Another group were just sitting down to supper here, but, worn out as they were, they all went on to Dunchurch, where Sir Everard Digby awaited them.

The boys kept upon their track as best they

might. They found that the eight men, with their servants, had made for Warwickshire. They must now have given up the pursuit had they not fallen in with a company of country people, under the sheriff's leadership. The news had come down from London, and these men were looking for the fugitives. Jan was aghast at his friend's recklessness, but Giles had altogether lost his head. Spurring his tired horse to the officer's side, he begged:—

"Oh, sir, mount us and let us go with you! We can identify every one. We have heard them plan this flight, and know whither they go. Take us with you, and you will see that we speak the truth."

"Horses for these youths!" cried the sheriff. "And now ride on."

They were led across Worcestershire also. On the evening of the 7th they traced their prey to a house at Holbeach. Here, it was evident, they were determined to make a stand, and hold out the place against attack. The sheriff of Worcester was roused, but deemed it wise to wait till day for action. Giles and Jan rode restlessly around the house watching for signs of life within. They saw a troop of servants steal away. Then came out a gentleman,—it was the master of the house,—followed by Sir Everard.

Directly afterwards there was a tremendous noise. A huge bag of gunpowder flew up through the roof. There had been an explosion in the house. It was learned later that there was an accidental discharge of drying powder. Several men were injured. Robert Winter, wild with horror, rushed out of doors and into the neighboring woods.

At noon came the pursuers. The sheriff, in a loud shout, demanded their surrender. Catesby looked down from a window and returned a defiant answer.

"Fire the buildings," called the sheriff to part of his men. To the rest he gave the order, "Storm the gateway," and they pushed forward.

The entrance doors flew open. Out into the courtyard marched Catesby, Rookwood, Thomas Winter, the Wright brothers, and Percy. They were armed with their swords, but had no opportunity to use them. Winter was shot at once in his right arm. Catesby sprang to his side.

"Stand by me, Tom!" said he. "We will die together!"

They placed themselves back to back.

There was another shot, and another. Two bullets from the same musket had pierced them both through the body. Those nearest the house saw Catesby creep back on his hands and knees to the hall. He grasped the image of the Virgin that looked down on the bloody scene. He fell over and died holding it to his breast.

Percy was fatally wounded. The Wright brothers were both killed. Rookwood was run through the body by a pike, and had a broken arm. He was captured in the rush from the courtyard. He lived to regard his companions, who perished in the assault upon Holbeach, as more fortunate than he. For his own end was certain. Not two months later he suffered the fate of a traitor.

CHAPTER XI

PRINCE HENRY AND CAPTAIN SMITH

THE servant at their tutor's lodgings came in about this time with a message.

"There is one Dame Tryon without," he announced. "She asks for Master Valentine. She has a child with her."

Giles looked at his friend. "It is Nurse Janet," he said, "and little Meg. What can be the matter?"

He went into the passage. His old nurse stood waiting for him, with Meg clinging to her cloak. As the brother stooped over the child he asked:—

"What brings thee here, Janet? Naught amiss, I trust."

For answer she handed him a pheasant's feather.

His cheek paled. "Whence came this?"

"A groom stopped me as my little lady and I were taking our walk in the lane at sunset. He had horses ready. He bade me mount and lead him to ye, an I loved my old mistress's children. What could I do but come? When we reached the house he gave me this. I was to tell you a boat lay in the stream, and a barge was ready off St. Katharine's Wharf to set sail. Do you understand, Master Giles?"

The woman looked at him piteously. She had all sorts of dark forebodings.

"Ay," said Giles quickly. "I understand."

He went straight to Jan with the intelligence. They flew about the room, collecting their small treasures. There was no time for talk; there was no possibility here of a trap.

Giles wrote two hasty notes, — one to be given to his tutor, the other to be sent out to the family at the Grange. Then they joined Dame Tryon. Giles took his sister in his arms and they hurried down the stairs.

Out in the street the groom still waited. The horses had disappeared. He approached Giles, removing his broad-brimmed hat. His bow was so low, and his cloak so muffled about his chin, that his face was still concealed.

"A vessel sails to-night," said a disguised voice, "for Ostend. Passage has been engaged for a party of four. Are ye ready to embark?"

"At whose suggestion?" Giles demanded.

There was a light laugh underneath the broad-brimmed hat, — a laugh that had something vaguely familiar in its tones. Then the disguised voice went on: —

"Heard ye never of friends at court? Ah!" more seriously. "His Majesty hath been informed, and it likes him not, of your connection with this plot, but you have true hearts to rely upon in the very shadow of the king's displeasure. Will you place your dependence upon them?"

Giles glanced towards his companion. Jan returned the look. "Yes," said they both.

The groom fell respectfully behind them on the walk towards the river.

"Where have I heard that voice before?" mused Giles. "It is feigned, yet it is that of some one I have known. Who is it, Jan?"

"I have no idea," was the answer. "There is nothing to recall any one whatsoever to my mind."

They spied a boat lying out in the Thames, and a slim little figure waiting for them on the bank. He motioned to the oarsmen, who approached. Then he stepped close to Giles. It was George Earl.

To Giles's boundless astonishment he threw

both arms about him and sobbed upon his shoulder. "Should they seize thee yet!" he cried. "Dear, dear lad, make haste and away!"

"Peace, George," quoth the groom impatiently. "Thy worry may work the very mischief thou fearest. Here, fellows!" The hoarse, unnatural tones had been forgotten in the outburst. They were resumed for the boatmen's benefit. "Take the woman and the child on board with ye."

Giles could not repress a smile to see how the servant gave orders like a lord. He had penetrated the secret now. He saw through the youthful freak of the heir to the throne. In the bustle he caught Henry's hand. It was snatched away, but not before he had raised it to his lips.

"My prince, what have you done for me?"

Henry's eyes were fastened upon Jan climbing down into the boat. He wrung Giles's fingers in his hearty grasp.

"Thou wert ready to save my life from peril at Winchester. This is only fair return, — for me and for Earl, remember."

George and his old enemy exchanged a murmured farewell. The two upon the embankment watched them, waving a last greeting, while the little craft dropped down the stream. They arrived at the waiting barge, where they were evidently expected. They were taken on board. The anchor was weighed. For the first time the two boys breathed freely.

It was only when the passing dread of capture was gone that they began to contemplate a future which, in truth, was none of the brightest. From Ostend, that port riddled by the Spaniards five years before, they must seek the Chapelains at Sluys, across a country desolated by the long war. They would be incumbered in their movements by the presence of a woman and a helpless child. After Jan's uncle was reached, they could not foresee their next step. He of course could take charge of Meg and her nurse. But the boys had no desire to return with him to Paris.

"What I should like best," said Giles, "would be to fight under Prince Maurice, as my father did before me."

"And my father," Jan rejoined. "Yes, if my uncle would consent to that, we should know what to do. But we are so young!"

"So young for what?" asked some one.

They were lying on deck in the sun, their backs set against a coil of rope, their eyes strained to catch the last glimpse of the English coast. Another passenger had been pacing up and down before them. Their discussion was so earnest that they had paid no heed to him. Now he paused beside the friends, and they stared up, startled, into his smiling face. He was a fine-looking man, though weather-beaten and scarred. His smile was kindly and interested.

"What are ye too young to do?" he demanded again.

The boys scrambled into more respectful attitudes.

"To fight for the Netherlands, sir," said Giles.

The stranger seated himself beside them on the coil of rope.

"You might be admitted on a war vessel," he suggested, with instant sympathy. "Would ye fancy an ocean life?"

"Oh, sir, it would be the very thing!"

"Ye are about the same years, are you not?"

"There are only four months between us. We are each thirteen."

"Ay, I guessed right. I was thirteen

when I quitted my master in London and ran away to sea."

The boys looked at him. "Had you many adventures, sir?"

Their new acquaintance laughed outright.

"Some few," he said. "I have been in France and the Low Countries, in Italy and Egypt. I have fought the Turks in Hungary, and conquered the Pagans in single combat. I have been slave to the Bashaw of Nalbrits, and escaped from his tyranny as by a miracle. I am just returned from the wars in Morocco, and have lifted my battle-axe in Spain. Yea, lads, you say truly I have had my share of adventure, when it comes to that."

The boys' eyes shone. Their breath came quicker. "Tell us more," pleaded Giles.

"No more of my past. I will tell thee what I plan now. I go to the Netherlands, to seek a friend, one Henry Hudson, with whom I hope to arrange for sailing in the Western seas. Thou hast heard the tales of the Spaniards' prizes? Of the treasure they find in the Indies?"

"Ay, that have we." Jan sprang to his feet. "Oh, sir, take us with you!"

"No, no."

Giles joined in the entreaty.

"'T is not to be thought of," answered Captain John Smith, for it was he. "Should your parents consent" —

"We are orphans."

"Your guardians, then: were they willing, I would not subject ye to the hardships and the chances of such a life. Nay, nay. Wait a few years. There will be opportunities, no lack."

He eyed the disappointed countenances with considerable compassion. "This I will do," he said. "I will speak of ye both to Hudson. I will bear you in mind myself. Should I make a later voyage, or should my friend, when you are grown but a little older, — and, it may be, wiser, — I will surely send ye word. You shall have your chance to go with me then."

This was far from contenting them, but they gave him their names, and told him where trace of them could always be obtained.

"You will make the right sort of pioneers, I can see that," said Captain Smith consolingly. "All in good time, my lads. But I deemed ye both eager to join the forces of the States General. Why this change of mind?"

Jan tried to explain. "It is my country,"

said he, "and my father died in its defense, as did Giles's, though he was an Englishman. Of course we would defend it, too. Still, men say the war is drawing to a close. And oh, sir, a new life in a new land,— that is the best fate of all."

"I agree with thee." The man's eyes kindled, too, at the ardent tone. "Thou 'rt right. There's naught like that in this world. I hope it will be the lot of ye both."

"It shall be!" Giles cried. "I sicken when I think of England tangled in countless plots; of the Low Countries and of Germany, prostrate under the weight of conflict; of France with its religious factions. I long to live my life in a new, free world, and shape it for myself."

"We two together," said Jan, clasping his hand.

The man smiled gently at their enthusiasm. "You will win your desire some day," he assured them, "if you desire it with all your heart."

At Ostend they parted from their new friend, but not before he had given them invaluable aid, from his varied experience and his knowledge of the Netherlands, as to their further journey. They saw all about them, at the seaport, relics of the hideous siege. The country through which they now traveled showed signs everywhere of a generation of war. Yet what a marvelous land it was! These fields of rich grass supported oxen of fabulous weight, and sheep and calves without number. Wherever the natural fertility of the Netherlands had not been frustrated, for the time, by troops of soldiers and by battle, the travelers could bear witness, even in these dismal times, to the prosperous industry of its inhabitants.

So they arrived at Sluys. Poor little Meg was delighted by the sight of Jan's sister. Giles thought Annemie grown prettier than ever. She was but one year his junior, and resembled her French mother in her gayety and her dark-eyed beauty, as Jan exactly reproduced his father's strong Dutch features. Mme. Chapelain gave the young people a motherly reception that comforted Giles in regard to his sister's future care. Her husband was absorbed in his own affairs, but more careless than selfish, or indifferent to his ward's best interests.

He was soon to return to France, the service which had brought him hither having been successfully performed. He listened, however, attentively, to the boys' plans, and was somewhat influenced by them.

"I see no reason," he said reflectively, "why you should not strike a blow in behalf of the poor Netherlands. Young as you are, you have proved yourselves brave and apt. I will see what can be done: I have an acquaintance with the envoy in Paris, who gave me a letter to his father, Recorder Aerssens, at the Hague. I have used it for myself. Now I will use it for you. You shall go to him, and offer your services. He can best put you in the way of seeing a little gunpowder burned. I agree with you, lads, that there is no education, in these times, like a taste of warfare. Aerssens will manage that you have it."

It was nearer to them than the Hague, but this they did not imagine. While they all lingered on at Sluys, there came an adventure which Giles was not to forget, and which Jan never ceased regretting did not fall, in part, to him to share.

CHAPTER XII

THE TOWN CLOCK AT SLUYS

IT was a lovely night in June. Giles could not sleep, although he could give no reason for his wakefulness. He counted hour after hour by the tall clock on the staircase, outside his room. He listened enviously to Jan's regular breathing. He tossed and turned, and sprang from his bed to walk up and down the little room, hoping thus to induce drowsiness.

The night was drawing towards dawn, and he had scarcely closed his eyes.

"It is clear and calm outside," he mused, drawing the spotless curtain to peer from the window, "or I should think it must be thunder in the air that has so wrought upon me. Plainly, it is of no use to try to rest. I shall dress quietly, and steal out of the house. Perhaps a long stroll through the peaceful streets will be the best cure for my wretched excitement, after all."

No sooner thought than done. He pulled

on his clothes, and took a last look at his sleeping comrade, with the reflection: —

"Poor fellow! It would be barbarous to wake him, or how he would enjoy a midnight prowl!"

He glided softly down the stairs, pushed the bolt quickly, and let fall the chain. In another instant he stood in the street outside.

He had no definite plan for a walk. He rambled about altogether at random. Only the night before, he had overheard Monsieur Chapelain discussing with a friend the absurd rumor that Du Terrail was contemplating an attack upon the town. Both had laughed at the notion. Sluys was defended by a chain of forts and water batteries, and by a magnificent citadel. It may be that, ridiculous as the idea appeared, it had had more effect upon one listener than he supposed. The remembrance of Du Terrail's project may have driven away his sleep.

Be that as it may, Giles was pondering it while he walked. Since the attempt must result in failure, would it not be a lively bit of action where all had moved tamely for so long? There was no danger of any repetition of the horrors of Ostend, for instance.

"We can repel them with the first shot," he reflected. "We can so silence them — *What is that?*"

In his aimless course, he had reached the vicinity of the western gate. He heard the stealthy tread of armed men close at hand. There was the undertoned direction, the hushed step of soldiers marching in silence, yet with the inevitable clanking of their weapons.

This could mean nothing else but mischief. What mischief, Giles resolved straightway to discover.

Keeping in the shade of the tall, peaked houses, moving like a very shadow himself, he crept closer to the oncoming troops. He could hear the drip of wet clothing, the muttered complaints of those who, he afterwards learned, had waded through the submerged land of Cadzand. They had stolen past the forts without detection. Their petards had forced a breach in the gate; through this, he made out, the intruders were pushing, two by two.

They had entered Sluys.

It was time for immediate action, and yet what could he do? All sorts of wild thoughts flew distractedly through Giles's brain while the men filed down the one street, and he lurked in the dark corner of another, watching them from this distance. If they would only speak of their plans! If he could tell what the next move was, he might do something — anything — to circumvent them.

And still if that speech should be in Spanish, or German, or Dutch, of what avail would it be to him to overhear? He understood nothing save his own tongue, and the French that Jan and he always used together.

At last one soldier ran past, with lightest step, and another, equally cautious and still more swift, came close at his heels. They were both Irishmen, and, by the happiest stroke of fortune, they addressed each other in English.

Giles thanked the Lord for what seemed a special providence. He craned his neck to watch the two men and listen to their disputes.

One was urging some scheme which his comrade stoutly opposed. "No, no," he repeated vehemently. "The first party that makes an entrance is to march to the opposite end of the city. When the town clock strikes two, there is to be a simultaneous attack upon all the guard-houses. The garrison will be cut down at one great blow. Not that way, I tell thee. Thou seest where the others are going. Ah, here comes our leader himself."

There was a little confusion. The men retraced their steps towards the latest arrivals through the narrow gap in the gate. Giles, in his corner, was left to himself.

Now he knew what to do.

Up the silent street he ran like a race-hound, away and away, his feet making scarcely a sound, his body bent forward, his hands clinched at his sides. The soldiers, meanwhile, were pouring out of the gateway, and proceeding through the cross-street, as he had seen.

He must reach the town hall and the clock. It must be — his failing breath grew fainter with fear — now very close to the appointed hour, the time for slaughter. That hour must never strike. This was the first duty. What lay beyond was to be determined afterwards.

He reached the frowning building, in its narrow, turreted solemnity. He was prepared for the barred doors. He smiled grimly to himself, while he dug his heels and toes into the smooth brickwork, and drew himself up to a window-ledge.

"I have had practice in house-breaking," he thought,—"at Vinegar House and at White Webbs."

He pried open the sash with his knife. He dropped down inside into a gulf of darkness. It was a long fall, and he bruised himself severely where he struck the floor. But he was on his feet in an instant, and groping his path through the room. Stairs were found after a sickening delay, and after more than one false hope. Every moment, every second, counted, and there were so many delays! He climbed up and up. Sometimes he could not touch the railing; sometimes he was not certain of his footing in that utter blackness. The platforms were only to be crept across on his face, lying at full length, while his outreaching fingers clutched for the edge. Should Giles make one false move now, not only he might be dashed to pieces in unknown depths below, but—and this was his first thought—the alarm would be given, the garrison would be slain, and the city would surrender to Du Terrail.

He had a general notion where the works of the clock must stand. He had seen its round visage often enough in his comings and goings past the hall. By and by he could hear the loud, steady tick that guided his dizzy climbing. There was a rumble, a premonitory growl, as it were, in the machinery. It was on the stroke of two.

Giles fell forward. He thrust out one hand and caught at something, he knew not what, for support. With the other arm he pushed away recklessly among the cogs and wheels. He seized the pendulum; he tugged at the weight. His fingers were torn and bleeding. He paid no heed to anything except this; he had stopped the clock. The signal would never sound.

A half hour later the governor, Colonel Van der Noot, was roused from his bed by a voice outside his window. He sprang up, rushed to the sash, and called lustily in return.

"What is it? Is anything amiss?"

"Hearken," said an English voice. "Do you hear the trumpets?"

Every one could hear them now. They were playing a Spanish air. It sounded in gay triumph through the Dutch town.

A shout clashed with the music. There was an indescribable tumult in Sluys.

The governor hurried into his clothes. Half dressed, he sprang down the stairs at a flying leap, and threw himself out of the door.

Giles hastened forward to meet him. They ran on together, the boy telling, in panting breaths, what he had learned of the enemy's movements. Fortunately, there had been such numbers of his countrymen in the Netherlands, from time to time engaged in the war, that many Dutch could speak and understand English. The governor questioned him closely. Twelve hundred of Du Terrail's troops had entered the place. They feared a possible ambush, making their progress through the town. They were ever on the alert for an onslaught. Their leader, with some of his men, had not stirred from the western gate. They stood there awaiting the sign for the attack upon the guard-houses.

The guard were in arms, and the whole garrison. From every house thronged men just awakened from sleep, but prepared for combat. Colonel Van der Noot was ready to atone, by his bravery, for the false security that had rendered the surprise possible. He led the irregular army, with hastily caught up musket and pike. Together they fell upon the venturesome band who had dared to break the wall of Sluys.

Giles kept close to the governor. He had only his knife for weapon, but there was no need for his offices. The intruders were repelled with almost ludicrous haste.

The gap in the gate had served very well to gain them entrance to the town. It was quite another matter when the panic-stricken foreigners pushed by each other in their endeavors to flee through the same narrow passage. It was a picture of frantic terror, of tremendous noise, of frightful carnage. Five hundred of the enemy were killed at the gate. Of those who managed to escape, the larger number were drowned, or smothered in the marshes that lay without the town on the road they had taken to win it.

Giles returned to a household all agog with the events of the night. M. Chapelain and Jan were away. Madame shed tears of pity over the boy's torn hand, and the terribly bruised shoulder that had received the worst hurt when he sprang down from the town hall window. His old nurse, and Annemie and Meg, treated him as the hero of the whole affair.

When they were returned and had heard his story, Jan and his uncle were equally proud of the exploit. The governor sent for Giles during the day, and praised the boy's forethought. He questioned him in regard to his future movements, and delighted the boys by saying that he remembered both Wilhelm Verrooy and Anthony Valentine.

"You are the worthy sons of your fathers," he said in faltering English. "If you and young Verrooy like, I will arrange matters for you. You say you wish to see fighting. You both bore yourselves well last night. I cannot place you on any warship, but I can send you — and I will — to Prince Maurice. He is gathering an army at Deventer. I will give you letters to one of his officers. Will that content you for the present, young sirs?"

Their faces beamed with pleasure. It was hardly necessary to answer Yes.

CHAPTER XIII

WITH PRINCE MAURICE

"UGH, what a climate!" exclaimed Giles. "I begin to wonder that you were not web-footed, Jan."

He threw aside his wet cloak, seating himself at the tent's opening before the glowing peat fire.

"You know as well as I do that this rainy season is no less remarkable to my people than to you." Jan was lounging, in a languid attitude, upon the edge of his camp bed. He spoke rather tartly. Giles did not notice this, rattling on with his complaints.

"Think of a fire at midsummer, too!" He warmed his hands at the pleasant blaze. "It is as cold to-day as it was when we reached the Netherlands last winter."

"And you've heard it said a thousand times," Jan retorted, — "the soldiers are forever repeating it, — that no such summer has ever been experienced before. It's as the commander said to some one last night: 'All the seasons have come together. One can't tell whether it is spring, summer, autumn, or winter.'"

He stretched himself full length upon the couch. "For my part, I don't see what you mean by grumbling about the cold. I am burning with heat, myself."

"Why, your cheeks are like fire!" Giles said, regarding him curiously for the first time. "Are you ill, Jan?"

"No, no! I feel well enough except for the heat. What are they doing outside?"

"They are all gathered on the river bank. If you really are equal to it — I don't like your looks myself — we might go down there and see the enemy's attempts to cross."

The war that had lasted for forty years was drawing to a close. Its cost to the Netherlands, in what that fertile land had suffered, might be readily seen and estimated. Its money cost to Spain was reckoned at more than $300,000 monthly. The Marquis Spinola, the great Spanish leader, had been very ill. It was hoped that the Dutch would strike decisively, and end the contest, during his enforced absence from the field of action. But Holland's coffers, too, were almost emptied. Prince Maurice was hampered by lack of money and of soldiers. Another delay was caused by a dispute between Henry Fourth and the Duke of Bouillon. It was relative to this last matter that M. Chapelain had visited the Netherlands.

Early in June, Spinola arrived in Brussels. Assembling a large force, he divided it into two parts, one of which he gave to the command of Bucquoy, with 10,000 foot, 12 guns, and 1200 cavalry. This army reached Mook, on the Meuse, on the 18th of July. Spinola on the same day occupied Goor, in Overyssel, with 11,000 infantry, 2000 horse, and 8 guns, having crossed the Rhine at the redoubts of Ruhrort. But his plans to repeat his campaign of 1605 were frustrated by the weather, at which Giles had just now been railing. The roads became rivers, and the rivers lakes. Friesland was an impassable bog. Turning away from the east, he set out for the west, in execution of a plan which he had long had in mind.

The Yssel and the Waal rivers formed, as it were, two moats on the sides of a vast natural fortress guarding Utrecht, through which lay the route to Holland and Zeeland. Could Spinola but obtain the control of those two streams, he might yet, by the invincible position he would then hold, put an end to the Dutch rebellion at one stroke. Should he pass the rivers, he could bring his two forces together and the thing was done.

The importance of every movement at this juncture was fully appreciated upon both sides. The defense of the Waal had been given by Maurice to Warner Du Bois, with 7000 men. They were to prevent the passage of Bucquoy's troops. He himself was pitted against Spinola.

Jan's uncle had taken his family with him and gone back to France. There was a new sense of desolation when the friends watched their departure, and felt that, through their own deliberate choice, they were turned out upon the world. Mme. Chapelain assured them of the welcome they would find in Paris at any time they chose to claim it. The boys bade them all farewell, and then set out for Spardorp and Du Bois, to whose protection the governor of Sluys had commended them. And thus, on this wet summer day, that might, so far as weather was concerned, have been midwinter, they were spectators of the last land action in the revolt of the Low Countries.

When the two reached the river, they

beheld its yellow, swollen tide rolling upon a scene of most curious interest and activity. Armed vessels dotted its waters; armed men lined the banks like a wall. There was a dead silence among the watchers.

Upon the opposite banks one Pompeio Giustiniani was making preparations to cross the stream. A number of barges set out from shore. The Dutch noted eagerly the approach of the boats. It was obvious what they meant to do. As they drew nearer, it could be seen that they were full of troops.

"Huzza!" cried Jan.

He tossed his cap into the air. He had noticed the first boat slacken its speed. He saw the boatmen turn its course. The commander pushed forward and began an agitated remonstrance. He waved his hand towards Du Bois. They could catch the sound of his loud tones in his effort to cheer his men, and impel them on in the dangerous struggle for victory. Through the dropping rain, the whistle of the bleak wind, the rushing of the mighty river, the imploring, cajoling, threatening voice was wafted to the bank of the Waal. The solid ranks of men waited the result in dogged determination, their eyes fastened upon the wavering line of boats.

"Huzza!"

Jan's cry was caught up from a thousand throats. The first boat fell away. It dropped down the stream. The next, and the next: one by one, the advancing enemy beat the same retreat. Upon the pretext that the current here was too strong for them, they resisted every entreaty or command. Gradually they stole back to their comrades upon the shore.

An ear-piercing shout of derision followed them as they went. A Spanish officer in the last of the straggling line shook his sword in impotent wrath at the Hollanders.

Upon the Yssel, Maurice was keeping the same effective guard. In vain did the cunning Spinola move from point to point, watching his chance to break through the line of forts hastily thrown up by the stadholder. There was no weak spot. It was all defended beyond surprise.

"It is like a cat and a mouse," said Giles, "only that in this case the mouse seems to have the best of it."

"The cat has effected something," Jan answered from the bed. "He has captured Lochem" —

"Pooh! what was that tiny town? There

was no glory, and not much profit, in taking a place, with next to no garrison, that surrendered without a struggle."

"I know all that," Jan pettishly replied. "But there is Groll, too. Spinola has taken Groll, and they say he is on the march to Rheinberg. Oh, Giles, how cold I am!"

His tone had altered abruptly. His lips became blue. His teeth chattered. Giles flew to his side in alarm.

"You are like ice," he murmured, catching the boy's hand in his. "What shall I do? I will run for help, if you can be left alone."

For he thought his friend was dying.

Jan made no answer. Giles looked about him distractedly. He flung every covering that was at hand upon the bed. He seized a can of water and ran to the fire to heat it. He really did not dare quit the bedside, but the measures he took were quite as effective as anything could be in the course of such a chill. He made Jan drink the scalding water, and put a bottle of it to his feet. In his hurried search for another can, a small packet fell out of the doublet he had tossed aside.

Some recollection, vaguely distressing, was roused by its sight. Giles knit his brows: why did the squarely folded paper bring up to his mind another time of illness and of harassment?

"I have it!" he cried, relieved. "It was one day at York, in the course of the royal progress. How long ago it seems! My guardian was taken down with a sickness like this, and Sir Walter Raleigh heard of it. He sent us, through his Majesty's surgeon, a powder that, he said, the Indians use and find that it works marvels. Dear Jan, it is Providence that brings it to light in our need. I have found the cure! All will soon be right."

Much cheered at the belief, he mixed a draught and brought it to the bedside. "Don't refuse it because it is bitter," he begged. "I remember the outcry Sir Robert made. He said the cinchona was worse than the chill."

Jan was too ill to listen to much of this harangue. However, he mustered the spirit to determine that he would show more fortitude than Carey. He swallowed the dose at a mouthful, and lay back upon his couch.

A shadow darkened the tent opening. Giles looked up from resettling his patient under the pile of clothes. Warner Du Bois stood looking in upon them. Behind him, and glancing over his shoulder, was another warrior. He was clad in a complete suit of armor, and carried a helmet, with waving orange plumes, in his right hand. Giles noted abstractedly his fair, round face, his large blue eyes, the scanty locks that crowned his head. He bowed to the two men, and moved aside as they entered the tent.

"What is the matter here?" asked the stranger in Dutch.

Du Bois hastily interposed. He explained that Giles was an Englishman. The boy heard his name used, and his father's. A pleasant smile crossed the soldier's face. He held out his hand, saying in English:—

"I remember Anthony Valentine well. I am glad to meet his son in the field where he died in our behalf. For his sake I would do aught that I could for you. What is wrong here?"

He approached the bedside. Du Bois whispered to Giles:—

"It is the prince."

Jan answered the kindly questions as well as his miserable condition would permit. Maurice listened attentively. Giles stepped forward.

"It has been so with him," he said, "ever since we reached the Waal. First a fever, and then a chill. He has not been able to escape one or the other, though none ere this hath been so severe."

"Ay, ay, I see," the stadholder replied. "We must get him out of this quagmire; that is the first thing. Then — a sea voyage would be the surest remedy of all." His quick gaze, roving from one face to the other, caught the expression of pleasure that crossed them both. "You would like that better than sitting in this bog?".

"Oh, sir, it is the wish of our hearts to embark on a war vessel and see action upon the water."

"Would that all desires could be so easily gratified," said Maurice. He glanced towards Du Bois. "Admiral Haultain," he continued, "is to sail but shortly for the Spanish coast to pick up a golden prize. 'T is the very adventure in which these youths would delight."

He spoke in his own tongue. Jan answered him. His chill was departing. His eyes sparkled so brilliantly that his friend feared the fever had returned.

"I should not ask more of fortune," said he. "And Giles, here, is of the same mind. If the admiral will take us" —

"The admiral will take you," Prince Maurice interrupted haughtily. "I shall do my part. Come, my lad, you must hasten to recover sufficiently to be moved. That is your share of the compact."

With that he quitted the tent, with Du Bois, and left them to talk it all over together.

CHAPTER XIV

KLAASZOON THE MARTYR

THE boys were full of excitement, not only at the prospect of sailing at all, but of sailing in a fleet commanded by Haultain. They had heard, in the previous year, of his exploit off Dover,— how he bound Sarmiento's Spanish legion two and two together, and tossed them into the sea. They knew him for a cruel man, and they believed, with the general belief, that he was as brave as he was severe. They were speedily to learn the truth of this.

Nineteen war galleots of the first class and two well-equipped yachts comprised the squadron. The vice-admiral was Regnier Klaaszoon, from Amsterdam. "They say he, too, has the spirit of a lion," Jan informed his friend.

Jan was already much improved in health, whether due to Raleigh's medicine, or to Maurice's, could not be determined. Both were transported with delight as they coasted, day after day, along the shore of Western

Europe. A few months before, the admiral had made the same voyage for the like purpose, — to watch for and to overcome the outgoing Portuguese merchantmen, and the fleets homeward bound, gold-laden, from America. He had not effected much at that time. The merchantmen had unloaded their cargoes, and postponed their voyage to the East Indies. Nothing was to be seen of the American vessels, and he had lost six of his own ships in a storm. Now he was returned on a further search for the treasures of Mexico and Peru.

They learned soon that the treasure fleet had not yet arrived, and were constantly upon the lookout for the first sign of its approach. They fell in with several merchant ships which they chased into harbor. Two or three landings were made and a village was burned. The sight was horrid to Giles and his companion, although they had been trained in a rough school of constant conflict.

Then fell a heavy storm. It lasted a day and a night. The friends were thankful that they were together, when hour after hour seemed likely to be their last. They were still more grateful that they had not been stationed on different ships when the second morning broke. Six vessels were gone.

It was a fortnight later. They had been cruising, in tedious monotony, off Cape St. Vincent, when Jan was sent aloft to scan the horizon. He shielded his eyes with his hand, and gazed searchingly out into the west. Those on the deck awaited the result of this oft-repeated outlook.

"They must come soon!" muttered the admiral, pacing up and down.

"A sail!" cried Jan. There was a faint stir. "Another! And another! The ocean is white with them. It is the fleet!"

There was a shout of rapture. Men flew here and there, in obedience to hurried words of command. Giles wondered that Jan tarried at his post. He looked aloft, and saw him still clinging with one arm to the mast, still shading his eyes with his other hand and looking out to sea. He stood, struck by a strange sense of something amiss.

Jan descended from his perch. He crossed the deck to where the admiral stood. That worthy's features were wreathed in smiles.

"What, lad," he cried boisterously. "Why that long face, as if you did not like the prospect? You saw the squadron?"

Jan shook his head. "It was not the squadron."

Haultain took a step towards him. His fierce eyes blazed with rage. He lifted one arm to strike the boy. "Have you deceived us?" he demanded hoarsely. "What does this fooling mean? Speak, rogue, or it will be the worse for you!"

Jan drew himself up proudly. "I reported what I saw," he answered. "But those are no merchantmen. See for yourself." He pointed to the distance. "They are Spanish warships, and they outnumber us three to one."

The admiral ran to the vessel's side. He could indeed see for himself. Bearing down upon them, now coming plainly into view, was the largest fleet that had sailed those waters in many years. Eighteen galleons Jan had counted, and eight galleys, besides a number of smaller vessels. It was a sight to alarm the stoutest heart, knowing their own resources, and seeing how terribly the odds were in the Spaniards' favor.

Haultain issued an instant order for a conference with his chief officers. The men stood meanwhile about the decks muttering to each other. They eyed the approaching ships, some of them with gloomy prophecies as to the result of a meeting; others defiant, or vaingloriously sure that the Dutch could follow up their prowess on the seas by a victory in the teeth of such forces brought against them.

The hurried conference was over. The officers hastened back to their vessels, the vice-admiral shaking his head in gloomy dissatisfaction.

"I don't like that," Giles said aside. Jan and he were watching the boat speed on its course through the water. "See how Klaaszoon sits in the stern, his head on his breast, his forehead set in a frown. He is displeased with the decision, whatever it may be."

"I am afraid we may all wish it other than it is," Jan answered. "You could see the spirit of the men just now in what they said. Flight would be cowardice, and yet it looks very much as if we were to end by running away."

Giles nodded. "Hear that," he whispered.

The order was sent forth. The fleet was to manœuvre for the weather-gauge. It would then be seen whether escape or contest was the next move.

"Discretion or valor!" muttered Jan. "As if a Dutchman should hesitate between the two!"

A gale sprang up that sent the unfortunate ships reeling beneath close-reefed topsails. It was some comfort to see that the Spanish war-galleys could not ride out the storm. They were forced under the lee of the land. " We have lost that much of the enemy's strength," quoth Giles.

" Ah, but the galleons ! After all, there is nothing like them for mischief. And see how they weather the gale ! "

The eighteen powerful vessels, reinforced by several great carracks, were bearing down before the wind upon the Netherlands fleet. They scattered right and left. The confusion became inextricable. The wind howled, and the spray beat upon the decks. Suddenly Giles seized Jan by the arm.

" These are no manœuvres," he called above the tumult of the storm. " It is neither more nor less than flight. And each ship is struggling to be the foremost in it. Oh, what a shameful day for the States ! "

With a gesture of overpowering despair, Jan flung himself upon the deck. He covered his face with his hands to shut out the sight of his country's disgrace. An exclamation from Giles caused him to lift his head again.

"Is it not so bad?" he inquired.

"Oh, that glorious Klaaszoon! See, see, he is standing fast! Jan, he is meeting unaided the onset of the Spaniards."

Yard-arm to yard-arm, a terrific combat followed. The unequal fight was too much for even the admiral's caution to witness. To the joy of his crew he checked the retreat, rallied five vessels — the rest were hopelessly scattered — and went to Klaaszoon's relief.

The Spaniards were discomfited for the time. The day was dragging to a close. At sunset, the vice-admiral's ship, crippled as it was, received a fresh onslaught. Those with Haultain looked to him to move once more to the former's assistance. What was their horror when the command was given, and ran throughout the remnant of the fleet!

"Crowd all sail!" the admiral had said.

"And Klaaszoon?" Giles turned his white face to his friend.

Jan was pale, too, with despair and rage. "Klaaszoon is to be abandoned to his fate, you see!"

The Dutch were displaying the seamanship in which they undoubtedly excelled the adversary, only to get as rapidly as they could out of the Spaniards' reach. They heard the guns from Klaaszoon's ship boom out over the seas as they disappeared in the twilight. The last glimpse any of them caught of the doomed vessel was one never to be forgotten. It was stamped indelibly upon the memory. Against the glare of the setting sun, its red clouds suspended over the victim, the devoted ship, hemmed in by its foes, forsaken by its friends, wrecked and broken, was fighting to the end.

Its future was known to the world soon after the admiral, who eventually fell in with the missing ships, brought back twelve of the thirteen, uninjured, to port. He had no very comforting reception. The States General made it clear, and the public agreed with the government, that, if the dozen had showed the courage of the one, the Spanish squadron could have been dispersed.

Nor was Haultain's lot rendered easier by the fact that he had only missed by a few days the American fleet that now sailed safely to land. He had lost his honor, he had lost his vice-admiral, and he had lost the opportunity to capture the richest prize that had ever been carried to impoverished Spain. Eight millions of dollars, cargoes of Brazil wood, silk, cochineal, indigo, sarsaparilla, and hides; there was wealth galore coming out of the west, and directly in his path when the Dutchman sailed away from Cape St. Vincent.

Meanwhile Holland was ringing with the tale of Klaaszoon and his men. They had never entertained the notion of surrender. They knew that escape was out of the question. For forty-eight hours they drifted about, the flag of the States still flying at the broken mast, a shot now and then speaking their undying defiance.

The ship began to sink. The Spanish admiral, Don Luis Fazardo, made a demand for surrender, with a promise of quarter. There were sixty men alive with Klaaszoon, and scarcely one unwounded. He went about among them announcing his plan. They must all agree or he would change his purpose. But they did agree.

They knelt upon the deck, the injured supported by their comrades. Klaaszoon offered up a prayer to the God who had led the Dutch, as He led the Hebrews in the wilderness for forty years. He asked Him to accept one more sacrifice in the cause of liberty. The others said a hearty and unwavering amen.

Then the vice-admiral rose and approached

the powder magazine. He tossed within it a lighted scrap of tarred rope. He went back to the group and fell upon his knees again.

There was a wild flash of flame, a report that shook the ocean to its depths. Klaaszoon and his men had chosen to give themselves into the hands of the Lord rather than those of man.

Two survivors were picked up floating about on the waves. The Spaniards brought them aboard one of their fleet, and questioned them in regard to what had happened. They were horribly mutilated. It was the final struggle of nature with which they told, and gloried in the telling, of Regnier Klaaszoon the Martyr, and the sixty faithful men who had gone with him to death.

This was the story that was electrifying the States and crowning the ignominy of Haultain.

CHAPTER XV

BEFORE GROLL

Giles and Jan were again with Prince Maurice in his encampment before Lochem. They were welcomed by the stadholder, with some trace of amusement at the evidence of their spirit and determination to be upon the scene of action. His face darkened when he questioned them about the happenings off Cape St. Vincent. It lightened again with enthusiasm at Jan's comment.

"Can those Spaniards think," cried the boy, "that a nation capable of such deeds as Klaaszoon's could ever give up the struggle for its rights?"

"From their own side the struggle is almost over," was the prince's comment. "My lads, you are witnessing the end of a contest that began before your fathers were born."

It was hard to realize this fact, while the fighting still continued on both sides as indefatigably as ever. Lochem was taken again by Maurice's forces after a five days' siege.

It was a dismal experience to the young combatants, little as the fierce old soldiers thought of such an event. About them lay the corpses of Spanish nobles, to be recognized by their perfumed gloves and their rich clothing. The unburied dead were a horrible sight. The forsaken streets, the departing occupants of the town, defiant in their degradation, touched the boys' generous hearts, and made them feel that first hatred of warfare that was afterwards to grow to a loathing in them both.

Maurice now besieged Groll with 15,000 infantry and 3000 horse. The strangely prevalent rains were still pouring down, although — and this appeared a mere freak of bad fortune — at the very time that he wished to cross the Yssel, a short space of dry weather intervened, so that certain of its shallows were not navigable for his transports. The long trains of munitions and artillery were dragged overland to Groll, whereupon the flood-gates were opened once more.

It seemed impossible to effect anything in such weather. Nor was there, apparently, necessity for prompt action. The Spanish forces were dispersed, and on the verge of mutiny. The Dutch felt, in a measure, secure. The siege was conducted after a leisurely fashion.

One November day Giles ran into their tent in a state of intense excitement.

"Spinola is advancing on Groll!" he cried.

"Impossible!"

"I wish it were. It only proves too true. The news has just arrived. It is buzzing about through the camp."

"And it is no idle rumor? There are so many rumors in the air."

"It is the truth."

Jan was off his couch and into his cloak in an instant. Giles regarded him in no little anxiety as they proceeded out into the storm. He knew his friend did not like to be questioned about his health. Jan acted as if this disease (of course nowadays it would be called malaria) was something girlish and of which to be ashamed.

"I fancy you would be as well," Giles commented, with a glance at the flushed cheeks and unnaturally sparkling eyes, "for another dose of Sir Walter Raleigh's magical remedy." The only answer vouchsafed him was a sort of growl of disgust.

They soon learned not only the truth, but further particulars of the tale that Giles had picked up. Spinola's army, made up of about seven thousand infantry and twelve companies of horse, was marching towards Groll. A morass lay in his path. Soldiers in noisy groups were vehemently proclaiming this statement, and that there would be time, before its passage was made, for the prince to complete his intrenchments. Work was begun at once, in spite of the deluge pouring down upon the camp.

Before anything had been effected, tidings came as startling and as true as the first piece of intelligence. Again Giles hastened to his friend's bedside. Again he roused him with —

"The Spaniards have crossed the swamp!"

Jan sat up among his wraps, for the poor fellow was in the agony of a chill. He glared at his comrade with an expression as much of anger as of disbelief.

"What silly tale have you brought me now?"

Giles answered, "It is worse than silly; it is true."

"I tell you this is absurd. The swamp is impassable."

"Yet Spinola has passed it."

"How can you be so positive? It could

not be done with such speed. Why, Giles," the invalid's querulous voice assumed a more persuasive tone, — " you know how little you understand these Dutchmen, — just a word here and there, — and how easily you might be mistaken in what you overheard. I know you have improved wonderfully in the language " —

" Oh, don't bother to flatter me," Giles interrupted with a laugh. " I own that I am at disadvantage with your countrymen; only unfortunately, it was one of the English soldiers who told me this."

" Then it is true? "

" Of course. But, after all, why should we not rejoice? I can't understand the way you take this news, Jan. And the men feel as I do; we have a larger force; we are on our own ground, which is partly intrenched. It is the golden opportunity to gain the decisive victory of the year over Spinola."

As usual, Jan was more cautious than his friend, although Giles was inclined to regard his present humor as the gloom of illness.

" We have the advantage in men," he answered. " But they say the prince has lost confidence in his cavalry since they deserted his brother at Mulheim. Then it is a fact that perhaps half of the infantry are disabled. This rain has bred one sort of illness and another, like flies."

Giles would not entertain for a second the notion of anything except glorious success for Maurice, and utter defeat for the Spaniards.

"We shall see," he said, tossing his head significantly.

"Yes," Jan added, in a very different tone, "I am afraid that we shall see."

At all events, Spinola was aware of the weakest spot in the rebel lines, and was proceeding straight towards that particular place. The prince drew together the wings of his forces, concentrating them upon the little town of Lebel. Now came a time of passionate suspense. The camp was full of desire for the battle which the soldiers thought was close at hand; another battle — and they all believed it would be the last — in the defense of the States. Sick men hobbled from their beds and declared themselves restored to health, although their looks belied their words. Gloomy spirits, that had sunken beneath the long-continued dark days and splashing rain, were high at the prospect of an easy conquest.

"The Spaniards are in our hands," Giles said jubilantly. "They are worn out by their forced marches through those fearful bogs, suffering from the same weather that was so hard upon us lying here at our ease. There could not be a more perfect chance for their destruction."

Jan said nothing.

The young Dutchman was not only thoughtful and observant, but he was a sort of pet of the prince's, who was especially pleased with the pluck that defied hardships, and even this persistent ill health, in a love of country. Such spirit was sure to commend itself to the stadholder, who often called the invalid into his quarters. They were far from comfortable, but, at least, better than those of the troops. Here Jan was enjoined to take such ease as was possible to the misery he constantly endured. Sir Walter's cinchona could not effect a cure while the cause of the malady continued. Jan's illness was sometimes tended by the hands of the prince himself. He gathered here and there, and put together, by combining observation and reflection, theories as to the relation of the States General with their commander-in-chief.

He saw that the responsibility of the campaign had been thrown upon Maurice in a peculiarly ostentatious manner. He guessed that the prince was less free to act than was generally supposed, and that, although Olden-Barneveld and some of his colleagues, who had visited the camp about a month before, had been inclined towards action, there was a restraint that was not comprehended by the world at large.

And the eyes of all Christendom were upon this little camp of Lebel. England and France, James and Henry, were watching anxiously for the next move to be made. It would be hard to find a parallel in history for that scene. All the partakers appreciated to the full the part they were playing.

"It is the culmination of this generation of battles," said Giles in one of their countless talks. "Philip is gone, and Alva, and William the Silent; think of all who have disappeared in the forty years of the Netherlands struggle! Everything points to the end. Prince Maurice has the last stroke given over to his sword here in the swamps of Zutphen. And the nations are afire to see him draw the blade from its scabbard."

It was a terrific shock to the boy that Jan raised to his a face that was white and set.

"I know every syllable you utter!" he cried; "and I feel its truth better far than would be possible to you. For this is my fatherland, not yours. Its fate and its good name must be dearer to me than ever they could be to an Englishman. Yet I am bracing myself to bear a stupendous blow."

"What sort of blow?" stammered Giles, completely taken aback.

"I cannot say certainly. I know this: whatever is done will be, not our commander's fault, but that of the States General. He is in daily correspondence with them. Every step he takes, or fails to take, is by their advice. We ourselves, little as we understand the workings of his mind, can see that many of their plans have been carried out by him sorely against his better judgment."

"But — Jan — you cannot mean — nobody could mean" — Giles was becoming unintelligible in his dismay. "It can't be that the government could counsel him to refuse battle now?"

"That remains to be seen," answered Jan coldly. But there were actually tears in his eyes.

"And the prince would bear all the censure of the lookers-on?"

"Yes, that is so. He will — he would bear the blame."

There was a tumult in the camp, — the noise of shouting. The boys looked at each other.

"That was from our soldiers," said Giles. "And it was not joy."

"No," Jan answered between his teeth; "it was rage."

They met a man as they ran out of the tent. He was hurrying past them, head down and face distorted.

"What is the news?" Jan inquired briefly.

He hurled his answer at them over his shoulder as he hastened on. There was an expression of fury upon his features.

"The siege is raised. The field is abandoned. Retreat is the order of the day."

He told the plain truth. Maurice broke camp, and led his forces to the village of Zelem. The same day the Marquis Spinola retired into Munster, having relieved the city. It was the close of the campaign. The last land battle had been fought in the forty years' war. To the rage of the prince's men, the execrations of his allies, it had not been the battle of Groll.

CHAPTER XVI

THE RECORDER'S GUEST

"It is truly an ill wind that blows no one any good," said Giles. "Even at the price of such disappointment, I am thankful that we are out of those sickly marshes, and have brought you safely to the Hague."

"And here," Jan answered, "I am recovering my health by the minute." He could bear to speak of his illness when it was in the past. He was marvelously improved already. They had carried M. Chapelain's letter, reinforced by one from Maurice, to Recorder Aerssens, who took them into his family at once. He encouraged them to believe that, if they wished for another voyage, they might yet see ocean warfare, and wipe out the disgrace of last September, when the spring should come.

They were waiting for this in the Hague, and learning something, in the agreeable life they led there, of the Dutch manners and customs that were almost as strange to Jan —

he had been so young when he was carried off to England — as to his companion. They were sturdy fellows, bearing privations without complaint. Still, it was pleasant to see prosperity about them again, and to indulge in luxuries unknown to them under King James's rule. Life at home had been one of magnificent dress, of lavish splendor. But Elizabeth was always cramped in resource, as well as penurious in expenditure. Her successor entered upon like conditions; he loved money, and he had not enough of it to spend. The people of Holland lived in comfort, for they used their incomes on such things as pleased them, and cared nothing for merely outshining their neighbors. They dressed richly; they ate heartily; and their homes were provided with innumerable niceties all new to the recorder's visitors. Spices for their food were one little item appreciated in days when there was no variety, and more coarse profusion than delicate cookery.

They were eating with boyish appetites, one day in February, when a guest appeared at Aerssens's dinner table. "Draw up, cousin," said the recorder heartily, after the first greetings were over. "The meal has but just been placed upon the board."

The new-comer was Werner Cruwel, a tradesman from Brussels, who had recently failed in business. Aerssens supposed that his doleful manner was the result of this misfortune. When his relative refused the invitation to join them, he was impatient with such excessive grief over what was past and done with.

"Cheer up, man," he urged. "It will do your affairs no good, but rather hurt, to fast because of them."

Cruwel paid no attention to this. "You have little idea," said he coldly, "of what is on my mind." He took a letter from his pocket-book, and handed it across the board to Aerssens.

The recorder's eyes grew big as he read. There was absolute silence in the room.

"What I have to tell you," said his cousin, when the letter was finished, "will wait till later."

He glanced significantly at the family. Aerssens nodded his head. When the cloth had been removed, and the recorder's wife and children rose, Giles and Jan sprang up to accompany them. Aerssens checked them by a look.

"You may stay, if you choose," he told

them. "The introductions you brought were vouchers for you both. Perhaps you will be glad some day to have heard my cousin's message. I think it will make history."

They sank back in their seats. The recorder addressed Cruwel. "This letter," tapping it with his forefinger, "purports to come from President Richardot."

"Yes."

"I can hardly believe what it appears to state."

"You can altogether believe it," Cruwel answered, "if it tells you that I am sent on a secret mission from the President and Father Neyen."

"That mission being"—

"A treaty for a truce. I have here a memorandum,"—he produced it from his carefully guarded pocket-book—"signed by the Marquis Spinola and by Father Neyen. They agree to a ten or twelve year's armistice, upon one condition only,—that the States abstain from Indian navigation."

Giles stole a look under his eyelashes at Jan. They had of late been hearing fairy-like tales of America. Their traveling companion, Captain Smith, had sent what was supposed to be gold-dust to England. Wild stories were afloat of his adventures with Powhatan, "the emperor of Virginia." The Netherlands were as greedy as the English for a share of these possible treasures. A West India Company was established where an East India Company was already in existtence. The boys were beginning to look forward once more to a journey to those new countries, — the land of the cannibal and of the inexhaustible mines, — if Captain Smith's friend Hudson were to sail again.

The recorder rose to his feet.

"I think it best," he said, "to confer with the advocate. With your permission, cousin, we will postpone this interview until I have laid the matter before him."

"It is as you please," said Cruwel.

"Would you care to accompany me?" Aerssens asked the boys. They assented eagerly.

Barneveld they found in bed and asleep. He was at once awakened to hear this important intelligence. It was rather amusing to notice the cool way in which Aerssens spoke of his relative. He said that he thought business reverses had changed the man, and, "in spite of his sly and lumpish manner, he is false and cunning."

His advice was for the advocate to question Cruwel before witnesses. Barneveld listened in silence.

"The prince must hear what he has to say," he declared at length. "And you shall be present. Of course you answer for these youths?"

He shot a quick look from Giles to Jan.

"Prince Maurice answers for them," said the recorder.

"Then you," — he addressed Jan, — "can be our messenger. Go to the stadholder, and tell him what you have heard. Ask him if he will question Cruwel in our presence."

Jan was elated by this responsibility. He faithfully discharged the trust. For reward, perhaps, he was allowed to be present two days later when Cruwel delivered to the prince, the advocate, and the recorder the memorandum signed by Spinola and Father Neyen, with another signed by the latter alone. In this the friar offered to make a secret visit to the Hague, unknown to any one in the States except those who now learned his design.

Maurice treated this last document with contempt.

"Tell Neyen," he announced, "that if he

would address me on matters of such importance, he must send me in writing a proposal that merits serious attention. This" — he flipped the paper scornfully, — "is apparently nothing save a trick."

This was the conclusion of all three men regarding the affair, even when Cruwel reappeared at the end of a week with a formal avowal from Neyen. He declared himself authorized to treat with the States by the archdukes, who promised to surrender all right to the "so-called United Provinces," but demanded to know what would be given in return. The prince and the advocate said to each other and to Aerssens that the archdukes might intend to recognize their freedom, and yet secretly do all they could to corrupt their government. War could be renewed after dissensions had been sown, and they would be worse off than before.

It was, however, thought best to treat with the friar. Neyen and Cruwel arrived at a village one and a half miles from the Hague. They were disguised as traveling tradesmen.

Since Jan had seen the recorder's cousin, he was appointed to accompany the carriage sent to meet these men.

"You Dutchmen hang together," sighed

Giles. "I wish I had your chance. Or — no, not that! but that there were two chances, one for each."

Although it was almost morning before Jan returned, he was awake to greet him. The messenger fell into the nearest seat, and stretched his arms in a prodigious yawn.

"Ugh, how tired I am!" he exclaimed. "I feel as if I could sleep for a week."

"Well?" Giles hinted.

"Well, I know you are curious to hear every word. Let me see, where shall I begin? I sat inside the carriage in state. There were two mounted musketeers on either side. I felt like a royal personage. When we arrived at Ryswick I gave directions to stop a few yards away from the inn. I proceeded there on foot, and soon found my men. They were dressed as burghers. The friar played his part well. Of course Cruwel was just himself. I spoke to him, and he recalled me without my credentials from the recorder. He remained at the inn. When we entered the carriage, Neyen was alarmed at the sight of the armed men. I told him they were an escort, and that quieted him. We drove to the palace. I took him by the hand, and conducted him along the corridors without a word. My instructions were to add to the impressiveness of those deserted halls, and I did so. He looked quite frightened. We reached an inner apartment. I knocked at the door. The prince received us standing by a table littered with papers and books. With him was the advocate.

"They both welcomed him cordially. Prince Maurice asked him how he dared to enter the Hague relying upon the word of a beggar."

Both boys smiled. They knew, as the friar had done, that Maurice alluded to the once scornful epithet afterwards adopted by a political party, which had become a stock name for the Dutch rebels.

"He answered," continued Jan, "that he knew no one who would shrink from confidence in so exalted and respectable a beggar. They all laughed a little. Then he produced letters from the archdukes. He said — this did sound absurd, although he acted as if he believed in it himself — that the royal souls of the writers shone forth in those papers. They had not a thought for their own advantage: they were moved solely by the remembrance of the tears of thousands of human beings reduced to misery. They cared nothing at all for what would be said by the kings of Europe as to their excessive indulgence. This was too much for the stadholder's patience. 'What indulgence?' said he sharply.

"The monk answered: 'Is it not a great indulgence to give up their inherited right to these provinces? To declare those people to be free against whose rebellion they have waged war that bade fair to be endless?'

"Prince Maurice took him up quickly upon that. He said:—

"'Our right hands gained this freedom. The archdukes have not granted it. We have bought it at the price of treasure freely spent, and by the blood of countless heroes.' I thought, Giles, of your father's life and of mine. They went to purchase Holland's liberty. The stadholder went on: 'All Christian kings, save him of Spain and his relatives, have acknowledged our independence. We ask no gift from the archdukes. We claim the recognition of our freedom. If they are unwilling to give it, we can still fight. They shall find, in the future as in the past, that we love liberty more than life.'

"Well, then they dismissed Neyen. I was called from my corner, and carried him off to the captain of the citadel, where he was given a bed in all comfort. What I want most now is mine."

The treaty was next discussed before the States General. As had been foreseen, public comment and advice complicated matters. Neyen went back and forth between Brussels and the Hague. At the former place, when the armistice was announced, it was received with anger by the nobles, and rapture from the common people.

This was in the middle of April. But Giles and Jan by that time were far away.

CHAPTER XVII

IN GIBRALTAR BAY

ONE day in the latter part of March, Prince Maurice sent for Jan and his friend. He received them with a jest. His face was bright and determined.

"Are ye still bent upon going to sea?" he asked them.

"Oh, sir, is there any chance," Giles cried, "of a voyage to the Indies?"

"Not yet. At least that is not what I had in mind. What think ye of an expedition to Spain?"

They gave a cry of pleasure that warmed the warrior's heart.

"That is the true ring of good metal," he said. "Ye are, then, wishful to wipe out the stain of Cape St. Vincent?"

"To follow in Klaaszoon's footsteps, if occasion serve," Jan answered with kindling eyes.

"There spake the Dutch blood in sooth. Yea, and you will have for commander another

Regnier Klaaszoon. Heard ye ever of Jacob van Heemskerk?"

"All must have heard of him," Giles replied. "Of his terrible sufferings in Nova Zembla, of his many voyages, of the Portuguese carrack, bursting with treasure, that he brought back to the Netherlands."

"Good! I am about to send ye down the western coast with Van Heemskerk."

When the boys arrived on board the Æolus, and were summoned to the admiral's presence, they could hardly believe that the fine-featured, fair-haired man, with the gentle manner and quiet dress, who was laughing softly over the prince's letter, was the valiant sailor of whom they had heard so much.

He congratulated them, as if their warlike ardor was rather a joke, on the opportunity they would probably soon enjoy. They learned from the men that they were bound to the coast of Portugal, to meet the armaments that were preparing in port, the American fleet that was expected, and the cruisers that should put out against the East Indian merchantmen.

There were twenty-six of the Dutch vessels, with four tenders. Their names were fierce enough, — the Red Lion, the Golden Lion, the Griffin, the Tiger, the Black Bear, the White Bear, the Sea Dog, among the number. Two of the other commanders in the fleet were familiar to Dutch history, — "Long Harry" of Amsterdam, and the admiral, called by his men "Pretty Lambert." Both were seamen as brave as lions.

On arriving at the mouth of the Tagus, Heemskerk sent a lugger, disguised as a trader, up that river to spy out the condition of affairs. The boys pleaded to be allowed to accompany the expedition, but the admiral refused.

"No, no," he insisted, smiling at their contempt of danger. "The prince gave you into my hands to see fighting, not, perhaps, to have your brave young heads popped off by a chance musket-shot on a scouting inland expedition. You will have action in plenty later on. Bide your time."

The spies brought back tidings that the Indian fleet would not sail from Portugal for months to come; that no returning argosies were looked for. The faces that had lengthened at this intelligence, brightened at the additional news, — there was an immense war fleet now in Gibraltar Strait. These galleons were set to intercept the Dutch traders which should enter the Mediterranean Sea, or sail along it, homeward bound, from the East.

No news could have been more congenial to the admiral. Here was an adversary worth attacking. He had rather scorned the idea of capturing merchantmen who could not resist to any advantage. The warships were in every way his superiors. All the greater the glory for him and for Holland — only that he put Holland first — if they did win. He never doubted that they should.

The squadron reached Gibraltar Bay on the morning of the 28th of April. The Dutch rebels had been victorious in the Channel and the German Ocean, as well as along the Indies. Now they had come to the very stronghold of the king whose allegiance they had thrown off, who claimed universal sovereignty on land and sea. His mighty vessels lay at anchor under the shadow of the fortress on the rock, — ten immense galleons, eleven carracks, and smaller war-vessels. Their admiral was D'Avila, whose son was captain of the flag-ship St. Augustine.

An order was sent out for all the captains to assemble upon the Æolus. Van Heemskerk addressed them, standing in front of the mainmast. Giles and Jan approached as close as they dared, not to lose one word.

"We are between two continents," he said. "Europe and Africa are watching what we do. It would be hard for the Netherlands not to win upon the seas. But you must understand that it is either victory or death. We cannot escape the one or the other. The enemy's vessels are greater than ours; this makes them more unwieldy, and the better targets. They have larger crews; our shot must take effect upon those decks that are black with men. We are good sailors. They are landsmen, upset by the rolling of the water. And now farewell. Remember that to-day may give our fatherland the power of dictating terms to the haughty Spaniards, and lay the foundations of peace with honor."

The speaker told them curtly his course of action. The Æolus was to grapple with the St. Augustine upon one side and the Tiger upon the other. Two and two, the Dutch ships were thus to attack the galleons, the admiral leading, and the rest following him.

The solemn oath to stand by one another was administered. The sentences had a peculiar significance to Giles and Jan, who hearkened to the pledge with a quickened remembrance of that cruel flight off Cape St. Vincent, and the last glimpse of Regnier Klaaszoon, his crippled ship lying black against the sunset.

The captains went back to their vessels. The fleet began to move forward. When D'Avila saw the advancing ships, he called for a Dutch skipper who was a captive on board, and inquired if those sail were his countrymen's.

He said quietly, "Yes."

"What can they be after?" asked D'Avila. "Why do they approach us?"

"I think it is highly probable," said Gevaerts, "that they are coming to fight with you."

The admiral roared with laughter. His captive stood in silence, waiting any further speech.

"Why, the St. Augustine alone," exclaimed D'Avila, still shaking with mirth, "shall sink every vessel in the whole Dutch fleet."

The skipper bowed, in the same odd silence, and went away.

There was certainly no lack of combatants for Spain. The admiral had over 4000 soldiers under him, besides the sailors. At the prospect of a battle with the hated Netherlanders, volunteers by the hundred, of Philip's noblemen, came out from shore to take a part in the humiliation of the rebels who had presumed to seek them in their very homes.

It was about noon. The Dutch were close at hand. On every ship prayer had been offered up: they asked the Lord of battle to defend the right, to deliver the enemy into their hands, or to grant them the death of honor.

Heemskerk led the way. He told his gunners not to fire till the Æolus struck the side of the St. Augustine.

"Wait till you hear it crack!" was his order.

He added, raising his voice that all might hear him: "One hundred florins to the man who pulls down that flag!" and he pointed to the pennant fluttering in the dying breeze from the mast of the St. Augustine.

D'Avila's laugh had been very loud, but perhaps there was not so much heartiness in it after all. He assuredly did not set about his self-appointed task of sinking the entire opposing fleet. Instead of that, he gave hasty orders to cut the cable of the flag-ship, and they drifted out into the bay.

Heemskerk's men looked at each other,

wondering what he would do. They soon learned. He issued a command, in his usual low-pitched tones, to steer past the two or three galleons between him and his victim, and went crashing against the side of the St. Augustine. The guns spoke out at the signal. Pretty Lambert saw what was expected of him, and brought the Tiger to the other side.

The flag-ship fired upon Van Heemskerk, but without doing a great deal of damage. She fired again. Giles was standing near the admiral when a cannon-ball whistled over him, so close that it made him fall back before its force. The next moment he wished that he had been struck, for it carried away the head of a sailor also in its path, and cut off Van Heemskerk's leg at the thigh.

A group gathered about their leader as he fell upon the deck. A gush of blood flooded the boards. His orange scarf was dyed an ominous scarlet. Captain Verhoef bent over the stricken man.

"Fight to the last," whispered Van Heemskerk. His face was growing ghastly white. Jan knelt beside him, supporting his head upon one knee.

"I will," the captain promised.

"And don't let the rest know that I am gone."

"No."

"You will win, Verhoef, without me," he said. "May God receive my soul!"

Jan made a motion to the captain. He sadly inclined his head. The dead body was laid upon the deck. Giles spread his cloak reverently over the still features, and crossed the hands above the orange scarf. The guns were firing, and the battle waged fiercely. None except those upon the Æolus knew that their admiral had been killed. The men on the flag-ship were mad to avenge his death.

A broadside from her did awful injury to the St. Augustine. When the smoke partially dispersed, they could see D'Avila's body carried below. He had not sunk the Netherlands fleet, and he had been slain.

Hemming her in, the Æolus and the Tiger were fighting their adversary. The Dutch vice-admiral had been prevented from carrying out the directions Van Heemskerk had given him. While preparing to lay his vessel alongside the Spanish vice-admiral's, he had been set upon by two galleons. Three of his comrades' ships attacked the enemy, whom he was obliged to ignore, as he fought on the defense. Our Lady of La Vega, after a sharp combat, was set on fire. The Dutch sails were burning, too, from their close neighborhood, and the three vessels drew off for a time, busied with extinguishing the flames. Meanwhile the blazing ship drifted about at random. From time to time a gun would boom out over the fiery deck. The men threw themselves into the sea. The ship burned on and on, till there was nothing save a blackened and smoking hulk floating on the waters of the bay.

The vice-admiral had a hard struggle with his two adversaries. One he finally managed to sink. The other he drove upon shore, wrecked and silenced.

Admiral Janszoon had set another ship on fire. This, also, was burning to the ocean's edge. Word finally crept to the Æolus that Long Harry had been killed. It was not a day of unmixed triumph for the Netherlanders.

The light from the burning ships went out. There was the darkness of night upon the water. And yet it was mid-afternoon of a bright April day. The clouds that obscured the sight were the smoke of battle. They put out the light of the sun.

CHAPTER XVIII

WHEN THE SMOKE CLEARED

JAN crossed to his friend over the deck strewn with the hideous litter of warfare. He placed his mouth close to Giles's ear, shrieking above the noise : —

"Captain Verhoef is trying to bring the most distant vessels into the action, — those that the admiral stationed this morning on the edge of the bay to guard against the enemy's escape."

"This morning!" Giles repeated. "It seems an eternity since then. Here they come! Can you see?"

The approaching sails were dimly visible through the dusk. As they peered out over the side, watching the advance, *something* happened, — they knew not what. There was a report, beside which all the former tumult was as silence. They were pitched with tremendous force against each other, and fell headlong upon the deck. At that moment they thought the end of the world had come. The foundations of the globe were shaken. They were tossed like a ball in the grasp of a giant. Nor was this the extent of the horror. The explosion had been caused by a hot shot from a Dutch ship falling into the powder magazine of one of the largest galleons. Every man on board was blown into eternity. Burning bits of the wreck floated about among the other vessels. Two were set on fire. Their guns went off with fearful sound. Then they, too, exploded. Once more Giles and Jan were flung about like cockleshells upon an angry sea. Gibraltar itself quivered. The whole bay was lighted by a fire as terrible as the darkness that it succeeded. No more hideous picture was ever witnessed in this world of awful deeds.

By the glare it was first ascertained what was the real condition of the opposing forces. Now one saw that every galleon was burned or sunk except the St. Augustine. She ran up a white flag that flew out almost piteously against the blazing sky where the sun was setting. Giles pointed out the symbol of defeat to his friend. Jan looked up, and then made a dash forward.

"No one sees it," he cried. "They are all

like wolves. Watch those faces, Giles. How shall we stop them?"

He could not get sight of any one in command to point out what had been manifestly overlooked in the heat of the victory that was assured. Despite the Spanish plea for quarter, the crews of the Tiger and the Æolus were swarming on board the flag-ship. The expression of the attackers was what Jan had described it, as that of animals, and not of men.

The boys could not join at night with their comrades in the rejoicing at the completeness of their enemy's overthrow. For the last act of that day's tragedy was nothing short of slaughter. It was a cruel age, of incessant contest, of men accustomed to bloody sights. But there was something so merciless, so wanton, in the brutal close of the conflict, that they said to each other: —

"Van Heemskerk would never have so treated a fallen foe. Would that he had lived to the end of the day!"

It was the remembrance of his death, of the heavy tidings that must mitigate the glory with which they returned to Holland, that hardened the victors' hearts. They fell upon the dying men who covered the deck of the

St. Augustine, and put them out of their misery, but not in pity. A trumpeter climbed up the mast and hauled down D'Avila's flag, the last one flying for Spain. Thus he gained the one hundred florins that Heemskerk had offered that morning.

A number of Dutch prisoners were found in the hold. They told their rescuers that twice a man had been sent to kill them during the fray, and each time the messenger had been struck down by a shot from the Netherlands' guns. This intelligence served further to infuriate their countrymen, already beside themselves, as if they had drunken bloodshed until it had made them mad. Some of the wretches who sought to escape their swords and muskets flung themselves into the water. Boats were let down, and rowed among them, the Dutch shooting, stabbing, and drowning by hundreds. The bay was full of floating bodies. Indeed, several thousands were thus put to death.

Among the papers of D'Avila, found when the St. Augustine was searched, there were secret instructions ordering barbarous persecutions of the Hollanders, and of those who should give them help in any way and anywhere. This fact had spread about among the fleet. It added the last touch to their ferocity. They understood what Spanish oppression meant, and they said they paid to-day nothing more than the interest on a debt of ill-usage borne by the Netherlands for a century.

It was useless to argue afterwards, or to point out that evil for evil is neither sanctioned by the Gospel, nor by the unwritten law that would show mercy to those who cannot retaliate. At the time, all that Jan and Giles could do was to take to a boat themselves, and, keeping among the swarm of desolate creatures swimming towards the shore, defend them where they could, and give succor if it were possible. They incurred the fury of other pursuers, bent upon butchery, rather than stand by, passive witnesses to the wholesale murder of helpless men.

The hulk of the St. Augustine drifted ashore after it had been abandoned by the Dutch. Strange to say, a handful of Spaniards remained concealed within it, after all the ransacking — in quest of plunder and of victims — that the vessel had undergone. When they reached land they set fire to the wreck, to prevent the Dutch again taking possession of her.

It was twilight, and the fight had been in progress since half-past three. All of that night, and until the next, the Hollanders remained in the bay. By unspoken consent, the boys kept apart from the others, side by side together. They saw the people of the town hurrying in terror away inland, carrying their household possessions.

"To think," said Giles, "that the despised Dutch rebels could spread such consternation on the shores of Spain!"

"Yes, my countrymen have many a time taken flight like that," was Jan's rejoinder, eyeing the busy scene. "We have won a tremendous triumph, as the admiral prophesied. The States can dictate terms to Spain. But what a price we have paid!"

Giles understood what he meant. His glance followed Jan's towards the spot where preparations were making for the embalmment of Van Heemskerk's body. The young Dutchman heaved a deep sigh.

"And if the glory were but unsullied by any touch of cruelty!"

"Don't be so cast down. War is a cruel trade. I never guessed how horrible it could be until I came to see a little of it for myself. One can't fight and keep one's sword free from stain. The main thing is to be on the right side. And we know that we stood there."

"Yes," said Jan. "I am heartily glad it is all well-nigh finished. I have had enough of it, for my part. I hope I am no coward, but I never want to besiege a town, nor take part in scuttling a ship again."

"Nor I. We have learned our lesson. But there are other adventures to enjoy. There is the New World to conquer. I would rather contend against wild beasts, and strange lands, and the obstacles of the soil, than against my fellow-men."

In this tremendous fight there had been only one hundred seamen killed on the Hollanders' side, and not one ship had been lost. Skipper Gevaerts observed, sitting in the forecastle of the Æolus and relating his conversation with D'Avila, that this was rather different from what the Spanish admiral had foretold, when he could hardly speak for laughing.

The fleet was now dispersed. Van Heemskerk had cared little for treasure and much for fame. The other commanders were not so high-minded. They had thriftier intentions. They sailed with their ships to the

Canaries, the Azores, and the coast of Portugal, first touching on the shores of Africa. Only two vessels were sent back to Holland with the news of their gain and their loss. One of these bore the body of their fallen leader. The other carried sixty wounded men. Van Heemskerk was given a splendidly spectacular funeral at Amsterdam, at the expense of the State. It was the first time the republic had paid this token of respect to one of her heroes.

The two friends returned to Holland at their desire. They were impatient to make final arrangements, and find a place — surely there must be one for them — on an expedition sent out by either the new or the older India Company. The prince received them, heard the particulars of the battle of Gibraltar in silence, and then he asked their plans.

"It is the old story," said Jan. "We want to sail for America."

"You have had enough of fighting?" with a keen glance.

"Yes," Jan answered. He did not explain, and Maurice understood.

"We all have," was his only comment. "This armistice is to last for eight months. During that time it is to be hoped that our deputies and those of the archdukes can arrange, if not peace, at all events a truce for fifteen or twenty years. I think we have fought our last for the fatherland."

He reflected for a moment before he spoke further.

"Don't resent it, my lads,—I trust you may understand me,—when I say you were too young for soldiers. You could not help shrinking from what is too often a plain part of the soldier's work. Rely upon it, you are not old enough for pioneers. Wait for a twelvemonth or two. Go to Paris. Stay with M. Chapelain. Study more. Learn whatsoever you can. No voyager ever knew too much of any sort of useful knowledge. In two years from now, if you will come back to me, I promise, if I am living, to find you passage to the New World. But not now."

"It is what Captain Smith said," Giles was forced to acknowledge. "He bade us wait."

"He was right. Be sure he has learned, in that Jamestown settlement of his, what poor work unlearned gentlemen make at colonizing. For the present I will help you in any fashion on your journey into France. God be with you, lads! I shall not forget you. I trust you will not forget Maurice."

CHAPTER XIX

THE KING'S SWORD

The Aerssens family bade the boys farewell, with sorrow upon both sides. They had been very kind to their guests, and Jan and Giles appreciated what had been done for them.

In the course of a week after their interview with the stadholder, they were on their road to France. Maurice was better than his promise. Guides, routes, and means of conveyance were provided rather in excess of what the young fellows would have liked. Their preference was for roughing it; but until after they crossed the border, there was no opportunity for any misfortune.

One lovely night in early June found them riding at ease through a barren country, a land that Sully's vigorous measures were improving, but still left much to desire. Their path led along a stream bordered by a strip of verdure. Great stones covered the bleak stretch on either side this greener spot. Here and there they could catch a glimpse of vines, or some such trace of cultivation.

"If we cross that meadow," Giles suggested, indicating the patch of grass by the water, "we may strike the highway. I think we have lost it here."

"Lead on," Jan answered.

Giles gave the spurs to his horse. To his surprise the animal snorted and backed away. It half turned. It seemed determined not to traverse the lowland.

"Perhaps he smells a wolf," called Jan, pulling upon his own rein. "Oh, look! Selim is performing in the same way."

His horse was rearing and plunging. It was useless to urge either one. The cause became apparent. Giles, in advance of his friend, felt a quick, forward movement. He slipped in the saddle. His steed was sinking beneath him. The frightened beast uttered a shrill cry, quivering in every limb.

"Keep back! keep back!" shouted Giles. "We are in a quagmire."

Jan was frantic with distress. There was no chance of assisting his companion. He had all that he could do in managing Selim. He could neither dismount nor guide the horse. Meanwhile, Giles saw that his was making desperate efforts to extricate his body. He floundered on, each second sinking deeper. His forefeet struck a slender vein of rock. He displayed the utmost intelligence, grounding those two feet here, while pulling with strength that was given to him for that supreme moment.

With the violent wrench he had jerked his rider safely from the bog. Springing across the brook he alighted on firmer soil, his sides plastered with mud through which the foam was oozing.

Giles breathed a prayer of thanksgiving. Jan joined in it with all his heart, as he wheeled his willing horse about and sought a crossing farther along the water.

They proceeded by the border of the marsh for three or four miles. Finally they struck a narrow path which wound on into a wood.

"I don't fancy this," muttered the careful Jan. "It looks like the hiding-place of robbers and murderers. Are you positive we are on the right road, Giles?"

"Oh, yes. This forest is accounted for. We must cross it on our way to the night's lodgings. Now I rather like it. The moon is rising; we shall be lighted. And if something happens, all the better."

Jan made a queer little noise in his throat.
"Something is going to happen," he said.
Giles listened intently. "It is rain."
"No, it is not rain. There is a combat over there to the left. Come on."

Jan gave his horse a slap with the reins and bent forward in his seat. The animal broke into a gallop. Giles followed close behind. They soon reached a small, green glade in the woods. The sound of striking steel grew louder. The moon shone down upon a singular group.

A little man in riding-clothes, masked and encumbered with a cloak, was backed against an oak-tree. He was set upon by three figures, all likewise masked. His sword flew hither and thither like magic, parrying the others' thrusts. The unequal contest was carried on without the exchange of a syllable.

Giles selected one antagonist and fell on him; Jan on another. The attacked had only one adversary left. Him he quickly disarmed. He had given a startled cry when he saw the two youths flying thus to his rescue. The opposing party still uttered no sound. Giles wounded his man slightly in the sword-arm. Jan forced his to the ground. He was the leader, for, as the boy raised him to his feet, he gravely and silently bowed his gratitude, and glided away through the trees. The others instantly followed.

The little man turned that eerie-looking black velvet mask full upon his rescuers. "To whom am I indebted?" he inquired in a rich and winning voice, "for this unexpected succor?"

Giles told him their names. He repeated his thanks.

"I trust you are uninjured, sir?" said Jan.

"Oh, quite. It was nothing, my good young friends. The whole affair was nothing. They dared not so much as wound me. They simply wished to hold me as a sort of hostage to certain desires of their chief's."

The boys felt curiously reproved. They knew that they had done the man service, and yet his manner betrayed annoyance, and — they fancied — a wish to get rid of them.

"Believe me, I am truly obliged," he repeated. "And now — I will not detain you longer upon your journey."

Thus curtly dismissed, they again set out to return to the path. On the way they passed two horses under another tree, at a considerable distance from the open space. A man, also masked, lay wrapped in his cloak, and soundly snoring beside the tethered beasts.

"What a mystery!" Giles exclaimed.

They had some difficulty in finding the road. As they jogged along it, their tired horses stumbling over every obstacle, the clatter of hoofs came from behind them. Two men rode gayly by at a canter. The smaller waved his hand and called out, "Well met once more!" as he passed them.

"It is our friend who resented our assistance," said Jan, watching his figure grow dim in the distance.

When they arrived at the roadside inn which was to shelter them for the night, he pointed out to Giles two horses tied near the door. "We have overtaken those men," he observed.

They found them inside the place, seated astride the rough benches, drinking with a company of peasants, who were enjoying the wine at the strangers' expense. One man was evidently a servant; the other was the boys' acquaintance of the forest. Such of his features as could be traced through the mask were the smiling mouth, showing, underneath the heavy beard and shaggy moustâches, the nutcracker jaw and the sparkling eyes.

Those eyes shot a lightning glance towards the new-comers. They interpreted it rightly to mean, "Silence!" That encounter was to remain a secret. The merry-making traveler invited them to drink with him. They excused themselves, saying that they required food first of all.

While the landlord was occupied in producing such fare as his house could boast, Giles and Jan were amused at the conversation that was going on among the party at the other end of the little room. They were discussing weapons. They thought the servant was nervous, and anxious to get his master away. The master lingered, playing some feats of swordsmanship for the simple astonishment of the peasants.

"Do you know the temper of a Toledo blade?" he asked. "See this!"

He drew the sword from a scabbard that sparkled with jewels. His man made a quick step forward. He had seen the lookers-on open their eyes at those flashing gems. The little gentleman shook his head at him laughingly. He fell back into his place.

It was a strong, steady arm that wielded the heavy blade. It dashed it again and again with the utmost force against the stone wall. Then the owner passed it about from hand to hand for inspection. There was not a trace of harm upon it.

"But my arm aches to the shoulder," said he, rubbing it.

Jan examined the hilt of the sword, rather than its point. So the swordsman noticed. He stepped hastily forward. He bent over the boy as if to recover his property. Giles thought he muttered something in the ear of his friend. The two wayfarers by and by departed, the servant showing signs of relief, the master gay and talkative to the last. Giles and Jan were shown to their sleeping-quarters. They were, for the first time, alone.

"What did that man whisper to you?" demanded Giles, kicking off his heavy boots.

Jan smiled mischievously. "He said, 'You have kept one secret. Preserve this other for my sake.'"

"What did he mean?"

"Simply that I had recognized — and he saw I had — the royal arms of France."

Giles dropped one boot with a crash. "That was n't Henry of Navarre?"

"It was no other man in Christendom."

Afterwards they heard gossip to which they

patched the incident of that kingly contest in the forest, and made sense of the whole. D'Entrague had set upon his Majesty, who was stealing in disguise to an interview with his assailant's daughter. Both sides were anxious to keep the escapade from the world. It became public through one of the attendants.

The next day our friends rode into Paris, — a very different Paris from the city of to-day. The streets were crooked, narrow, and dirty. The flimsy houses encroached upon each other, shutting out light and air. Armies of starving dogs fed upon the refuse with which the gutters were piled. The lanes that threaded the town were unsafe after dark. Henry and Sully were doing what they could to mend this bad state of affairs. They could effect but a small part of the general reformation that was required.

After all, Paris meant home now to these boys. Mme. Chapelain gave them each a motherly embrace. Her husband was hearty in his welcome. Dame Tryon wept for joy at the sight of them; pretty Annemie declared that she should scarcely have known her brother or his friend.

"You have so grown," she said, with a coquettish glance.

"And improved?" asked Giles, laughing.

She made another swift observation from beneath her curling lashes. "Well, yes," she answered. "You have become manly and fine, — Jan and you."

Two years went speedily and happily by. In the bitter cold of the following winter they heard of the meeting of Maurice and Spinola upon the Hoorn bridge, outside the Hague, — their first encounter in peace and in the interests of peace. The long-delayed arrangements were still postponed. The treaty for a twelve years' truce was only signed on the 9th of April in 1609.

Meanwhile the young Englishman and the young Dutchman were hard at work in their French home. They studied, as the prince had recommended, and observed and asked questions, and tried experiments in every direction which might prove of value to them in the land towards which they were always looking.

They relied upon Maurice's promise. It proved trustworthy. On a certain March morning Giles bounded into the room where madame sat at her lace-work with the two girls. Jan was close at his heels. They waved a paper in triumph.

"It has come! it has come!" cried Jan.

"We are to sail with Hendrik Hudson," Giles exclaimed.

Annemie burst into tears. Meg hid her face in her hands. Mme. Chapelain herself grew pale. "Oh, my dear boys," she faltered; "it is so hazardous! You may never return to us."

"Yes, we will," Giles answered, putting his arms around his little sister. "We will come back some day or other for you, too."

CHAPTER XX

ON THE HALF MOON

THE friends were interested in the bustling activity of Amsterdam. The discoveries made in the past century had opened up an enormous traffic, in which the Netherlands took the most important part. Amsterdam was their commercial capital. Its population had nearly doubled in the last twenty years. It was to gain more than double in the coming decade. Those who crowded into the city, to seek their fortunes, often built themselves temporary huts in the suburbs. A bit of land that a man's hand could almost cover was worth a ducat. The narrow streets, with their canal-ways, were alive with hurrying men, intent upon making money. The East India Company's house was pointed out to the boys, where they were to meet their captain.

This was a handsome, substantial building, two stories in height, with imposing gables and tiny-paned windows ornamented by cornices. The doors were approached by high flights of steps, such as one sees in the modern American city house of a familiar type.

When the boys drew near, two men were talking together in the court. One looked at them, said a few words to the other, and seemed to take his leave. He came forward and saluted Jan.

"This is young Verrooy, I think?" he said in Dutch.

Jan answered him.

"And this is Giles Valentine?"

He spoke in excellent English. "I am a countryman of yours," he went on, taking each by the arm and walking away with them. "I am rejoiced to fall in with two of my fellow-travelers."

"Are you Master Hendrik Hudson?" inquired Giles in surprise.

"*Henry* Hudson, yes. I have come to Holland to take the Half Moon upon this voyage, but I am no Hollander."

He was a handsome man, with wavy hair, regular features, and large, brilliant eyes. His manner, strolling along between the two young fellows, was particularly frank and pleasing. They were captivated by his condescension.

"I have heard of you lads from my friend,

Captain John Smith," Hudson went on. "When we met last summer in London, he asked had I seen aught of ye in the Low Countries. But I had been cruising wi' an English company, and so, methinks, I missed ye. I had scarce landed again in Amsterdam ere Prince Maurice told me of your wish. Ye have powerful allies, you younkers."

"And good ones," assented Jan heartily. "It was right kind of Captain Smith to bear us in mind so long. Goes all well with him in his Jamestown settlement?"

"Indifferent well," answered Hudson. "He is in England for a season. Court and people talk of naught save his strange happenings. Another friend of his and mine, one Robert Juet, sails with us in the Half Moon."

After they set out, the boys learned that Juet was the only other Englishman on board. The crew were Dutch, — a rough, wild set, from whom they kept as much aloof as might be. The mate was kind to them, as was the captain. The men quickly raised a cry of favoritism, and took a dislike to Giles on account of his nationality. He speedily saw that, if it were not for Jan, his life would be rendered miserable.

A disappointment met these two before

they had well left port. Since the prince and Hudson both understood their desire to visit America, they supposed that this must be the destination for which they had shipped.

"But what do you think the mate just told me?" Jan informed his friend. "This is nothing more nor less than a voyage of exploration, an attempt to find a shorter way to the East, either at the northeast or the northwest. We are bound for the coast of Nova Zembla."

"And not to the West at all?"

"No. It will be a polar expedition. The mate says that Henry Hudson knows as much of the northern waters as any man living."

Giles gave a groan of discomfiture. "I can't understand Prince Maurice," he said. "He told us in his letter that this was our long-looked-for chance, as if America was almost in sight."

"Nor can I comprehend our captain. He has spoken in the same fashion more than once to me."

Jan accordingly put a respectful question to Hudson at the earliest opportunity. Their leader gave a peculiar smile.

"Wait and see," was all he said.

On the little Half Moon sailed, through the

North Sea, around the North Cape, on towards Nova Zembla. Here Hudson had been directed by the East India Company to seek a passage by the north and east sides of the island. Ice began to impede them. Day by day they found it harder to struggle through its fields. Every hour brought new difficulties, while they struck out futile paths in the lanes of water between broad plains of ice that closed tighter and more impassably about them. The risk of loss to the ship was tremendous. The certainty came that they should be imprisoned in the floes if they did not beat a rapid retreat.

"It is what the captain has known all the time," Juet said in confidence to Giles. "The company were resolved he should try this course. There was naught for him but to essay it."

"Now will he strike out due west?" Giles questioned eagerly.

"What other way is there? Ah! here's the pipe for all hands on board. We will see what Hudson's plans may be."

The commander proceeded to lay them before his men.

"There has been a vast deal of grumbling of late," he said, "while we endeavored to push on in the way pointed out to us by the company whose servants we are. We have proven it to be impracticable. Two courses still lie before us. We can try to make the northwest passage, or we can sail farther south along the coast of America. I myself am confident that there is an arm of the sea jutting through the land somewhere north of the Virginia colony. I believe that it would lead us to the Indies. Men, which shall it be? I leave the decision to you."

They were all suffering from cold. They hated this strange, white region in its loneliness and isolation.

"The southern way!" cried every one.

Hudson smiled. It was his fondest dream to find that watercourse that would give undying fame to its explorer, and overwhelming advantages to the world, now all intent upon a "short cut" in the much-traveled road to India. He fancied himself a second Columbus, with, if it should please Providence, a happier fate. His views had not been attended to by the company. He had cunningly brought the crew to choose their way, so that nothing could be set down in their movements, whatever happened, as his own visionary scheme. He was sailing, at the demand of others, on his longed-for path to the west.

In about six weeks land came in sight, the fog-haunted banks of what is now called Newfoundland.

"We are still too far to the north," said Hudson.

Due south they steered. Day by day, in the pleasant weather, they coasted a vast tract of land that stretched out into interminable extent. Giles asked the mate once as to the colonists in this country. He was thinking of his idea, and Jan's, of some day finding a home there; of living a full, free life among those wonderful forests.

"Jamestown is no place for you," said Juet. "'T is choked full o' adventurers and idle gentlemen. Sickness and starvation, with bloody dissensions, are the tale of that settlement. The English have made, and abandoned, a footing to the north, in what the French fur traders, who are established there, call Acadia. The Spanish are far to the south. They have made other attempts, 't is said, to found colonies" (these were in Nebraska, New Mexico, Texas, and Utah). "There are Frenchmen not many miles from Jamestown" (in South Carolina). "Otherwise," and he laughed, "methinks you two could pick out a home anywhere in these thousands of leagues, and fight out possession with the savages alone."

Jan now joined them. "There is the usual complaining in the fo'castle," he observed, seating himself beside the others. "The men say that we have certainly reached that mysterious arm of the sea in the body of water to the starboard. Yet there are rumors that we are not even to explore it, but are to put about and sail due north."

Giles looked at Juet, who nodded sagaciously. "Ay, ay," said he. "The captain has found his bearings. He has been searching in the dark ere this. John Smith told him of this bay, — for 't is but a bay, mighty though its waters seem — and that 't was to the north that he had heard tales of an inland-stretching sea. We shall be upon the right road now, lads, — the road mayhap to India."

"I hope, for the captain's sake, 't is true," Giles answered. "For mine own self, I would fain tarry in this America."

"And I," Jan added, his eyes sweeping the lofty horizon, "to the end of my days."

"To have thy bones picked by cannibals?" Juet inquired with a grim smile. "Captain

Smith could tell thee tales of the natives' fiendish ways."

Jan touched his knife significantly. "I should die protesting," he answered.

"And in these times a man must fight wheresoe'er he be," said Giles. "There is no such thing as peace. Here, at the least, are discoveries to be made, lands to be occupied, homes to be raised, and, I trow, friendships to form among those savages,— cannibals, as you call them. They have not all proved unkindly to the Virginia settlers."

"New countries for the young," said Juet, rising to seek the captain. "For me, seafaring is a pretty trade enow. But may my frame be laid in the Limehouse churchyard at the last, an' it go not to the bottom of the sea in some storm or other!"

As he had foreseen, the course was changed. Jan told the men of Smith's directions, and of their leader's reasoning. They were satisfied in regard to this point, yet they resented the youth's superior information.

"The English are all for the English," they grumbled. "Why should you be in the captain's secrets because your crony is his countryman? Why should the fame of finding the passage be given to another nation?

Why did not the company send out the Half Moon under a Hollander?"

Jan knew that sailors were proverbially discontented. Still, he thought that their present attitude, among such scamps as many of the crew daily showed themselves to be, threatened harm to some one, — scarcely to the captain or to the mate, — but very probably to Giles.

One soft, bright day in the late summer, there was a cry from the lookout: not land, but water, was what they were seeking. After leaving the mouth of the Chesapeake, they had sailed in time past the Delaware, and yet Hudson was confident that this was not the much talked of "arm of the sea" for which he was in quest. Still they sped to the north. Now here they found the ocean ran landward into an expanse of bay.

Giles scrambled aloft for a further survey. He slid down to the deck to seek his captain. He raced to the cabin. Men were running hither and thither in no little excitement. Hudson strove to be calm, although his bright eyes shone like stars.

" 'T is the passage to India," Giles declared.

The fingers trembled that were rolling a chart. Hudson's tone was not quite under control. "I believe thee," was all he trusted himself to say.

On they pushed their way. A great river lay before them, lined to the west with a rocky wall. An island faced them, its green hills crowned with trees, and sloping to the water's edge. Masses of flowering vines flung a veil over the stately forest. Dashes of brilliant color threw out the blossoms against the verdure.

A little curl of smoke rose gently from a distant valley. It was like an enchanted picture of a fairy world.

"'T is a good and pleasant land," quoth Hudson.

As they thronged to the vessel's side to view the scene, a creature, such as none of them had ever spied before, marched slowly from the shadow of the trees. This was a tall, straight figure, of a dusky, reddish skin, clad in a scanty dress of tanned fur, and bearing a bow in one hand. A quiver hung over his shoulder. His black hair was braided on one side, and flowing loosely on the other about his stern, set features. He stalked on, unsuspectingly, to the water. He reached the beach. His sharp eyes were raised from the ground upon which they had been bent.

For a short space of time he stood still as a statue. Then he uttered a whoop that cut through the awful silence like a knife. He wheeled about, and sprang with the fleetness of a deer into the security of the woods again.

CHAPTER XXI

TAKEN CAPTIVE

" I WISH he had n't disappeared so quickly," said Jan. " Still, I suppose we shall see enough of the savages before we have made our way through the land."

" Lucky for us," growled one of the crew, " if we do not see far too much of them. I am afraid of the red men. Aha! he is coming back, bringing some of his friends with him."

A number of birch canoes shot around the end of the island. A supple figure sat in each, paddling rapidly in the direction of the ship. Meanwhile their hosts awaited them in the keenest curiosity. The natives climbed nimbly up the ropes that were flung to them, and swarmed upon the deck. The white men gathered around them, making signs, laughing freely, acting as if these were monkeys, able to amuse them without comprehending the contempt in which they were held.

" I don't like it," said Giles aside.

" Nor I," Jan answered. " This is their

home, not ours. They welcome us. I wish our men behaved less like the heathen, when they themselves have such Christian ways."

The visitors produced long copper pipes, showing the crew their method of filling and lighting them, and the tobacco they carried. The captain and mate had acquired the habit of smoking, perhaps from John Smith himself. Tradition says that Hudson introduced tobacco into Holland. At all events, many of the men understood its uses. They wakened a smile in the savages by snatching and puffing upon their pipes. Next, the Indians brought out baskets of oysters, and showed them how to open the shells. This was a very acceptable gift, although the receivers might have manifested less greed and more gratitude. Another present was not hailed with any pretense of thanks, except from the officers and the two boys. The Indians called them " pompions." They were great golden balls, that looked like a rare sort of orange. They cut hopefully through the rind, and bit generous mouthfuls from the core. But raw pumpkin was not at all to their liking.

" They appear very friendly," said Giles, " if the crew would treat them decently."

" At least Hudson will do his part," Jan

replied. "He is going to invite some of them to a dinner, and have his men show them tricks and sports. He thinks it is wise to be on good terms with the natives before he ventures inland."

All began well with this entertainment. There were songs and dances, and some simple attempts at sleight-of-hand that amazed the red men. A squaw was one of the party. She was ugly and worn, like all Indian wives, but her dignity and modest behavior were very pleasing to Giles and his friend, who waited upon her, and saw that she had a good position from which to witness the sailors' performance. She accepted their attentions in stiff silence, unaccustomed as she must have been to such kindness. They could not have told that she noticed any difference between their manner and that of the others. They had forgotten all about her, when she came up to Jan, as he stood at the outer circle of the gazers, and touched him imperiously on the shoulder. He glanced in surprise at her shriveled face. She lifted her hand in a beckoning gesture.

"She wants you to follow her," said Giles, who was watching them attentively. "Let us see what it is she means."

The woman led the way across the deck, looking back once or twice to see if they understood and were coming too. Behind a coil of rope she paused. She pointed at her feet. The boys glanced over her shoulder.

The chief lay on the deck. His head was pitched forward upon his breast; his arms and legs were twisted underneath him. He looked as if he had been thrown down in a heap and left there. The woman crouched beside him, touching his closed eyes, his mouth, and his breast. She raised one hand: it fell heavily back to his side. Her features quivered; her dark eyes, gazing piteously up at the boys, were like those of some harmless beast that had been trapped.

The man had been given strong drink.

"Oh, those wretches!" Jan hissed between his teeth. "Some of the sailors have been plying the poor fellow with *aqua vitæ*. How furious Hudson will be!"

"She thinks he is ill," said Giles. "It is hard to know how to undeceive her."

Another Indian stole up at the moment. He saw his chief's deplorable state. There was a loud, shrill outcry. In an instant the deck was alive with men. They flocked about the figure and the woman kneeling at her husband's head. They consulted together, eyes flashing and hands waving to and fro, or clutching meaningly at their arrows. Some one produced a string of beads and laid them about the chieftain's neck. They watched, apparently with high hopes for a time; but these had no effect upon him, although they were a valued charm. Then a warrior stooped over the squaw Winona, and asked her some question. She looked up, swept the circle about with her sad eyes, and rested them on one sailor's face. He shrank back, but it was too late. She leveled her forefinger at him, uttering a torrent of sound. The red men seized him. Their menacing gestures alarmed the entire crew. The accused, one Dirk Bloom, set up a vehement appeal for help.

Hudson looked perplexed, as truly he felt. He must protect his men. Yet this indignity placed upon their principal guest was supposed by the Indians to be of peculiar treachery. He crossed to Bloom's side, calling out as he moved: —

"For our lives we must pretend to do their bidding. Don't resist! Don't resist! They are five to one and armed."

He made rapid motions to the furious visitors. Happily the other white men saw what he meant, and joined in his artifice. He assured Winona and her adherents — among them her son, the young chief — that he himself would bind the offender (suiting the action to the word), and he gestured that death should follow, but not now, if they wished it.

They sullenly acquiesced. The body of the grossly deceived savage was carried to a canoe. His wife and boy followed, and the Indians all quitted the ship. Hudson drew a long breath of relief.

"We are not out of the scrape," he said to the culprit. "When I think what you have brought upon us, I am minded to string you up to the yardarm with my own hands."

Bloom muttered sulkily that he had intended no harm.

"You knew what a ticklish business our inland voyage would be, and how necessary was the natives' alliance. To think you should imperil all our chances for a brutal joke!"

However, on the following day, the chief made his reappearance at the Half Moon's side. He was rather sheepish, but good-natured as ever. His followers, too, behaved as if they had lost their animosity. Hudson did not understand the character of the men with whom he had to deal. He did not know that this affectation of forgiveness was part of their sly vindictiveness that only awaited a safe opportunity for revenge. He lost his fears, released Bloom, and he, the mate, and the crew speedily forgot the whole affair.

"But I don't like Winona's look," said Jan to his comrade. "I have seen her glance at Bloom when she thought no one noticed her; and I think we have n't heard the last of her husband's adventure."

The older men were not of his opinion. Preparations were making for the journey up the river, — the journey that, so they thought, would conduct them through the country to Asia. On the afternoon before that appointed for the voyage, Giles saw the sailor of the drinking escapade lower himself into a boat.

"Where are you going?" he called in his faltering Dutch.

"On shore," was the curt reply. He bent to his oars. Giles hastened to the cabin, made a hurried request for leave of absence, and was back again in a twinkling. Bloom stared in amazement when he dropped into the boat beside him.

"What is this for?" he asked.

"I am going with you."

"But why? I am sent for water. That keg," he thrust out his foot towards it, "is not so heavy as to call for two to carry it."

"Say, then, that I choose to go," Giles retorted.

Bloom especially disliked the young Englishman, who had not invariably concealed his hatred of the other's cruelty and coarseness.

"I don't choose to have you go," said he, laying down his oars.

Giles bent forward. "If you had seen," he began, "the murderous looks the old squaw has given you from time to time, I think you would prefer any companion to the risk of facing her and her people alone. At least she is friendly with me."

A startled expression crossed the Dutchman's face. He picked up his oars again and pulled along in silence. The boat ran up on the beach.

"Have your arquebuse ready," Giles advised, springing to land. There was a quiet all about them that seemed ominous. The waters and the shore were usually swarming with Indians. Their approach must have been observed, and yet there was no sign of life.

Bloom swung the keg over his shoulder.

He held his weapon in one hand as they walked across the pebbles. Within the woods a few yards, altogether out of sight of the Half Moon at anchor, was the spring where they obtained drinking-water from day to day. They entered the forest. Giles cast one look back at the ship. He was asking himself whether he should ever see it again. All depended, he was sure, upon the amount of gratitude Winona might feel for him. And, after all, he had done very little for her.

"Whatever betide, it was right that I came," he reflected. "Bloom's life would be worthless without me: that much I know. For the rest, I can but place the result in the hands of the Lord."

The tangled underbrush was something to which the Europeans were altogether unaccustomed. They pushed through it with stealthy tread.

"Do you hear singing?" whispered Bloom.

"Yes."

They came out upon the glade where the spring was situated. It was a wide, open space, and it was filled with Indians. In a hollow square they advanced towards a sapling post in the middle of the clearing. They were daubed red, and white, and black, and armed with clubs and bows. One of their number, the chief's boy son, carried a stone hatchet, which he threw towards the post. It clove and clung to the wood. Even these ignorant strangers realized that they were witnessing the signal for a combat, or a defiance. Giles swept the set faces with an agonized look. Winona was nowhere to be seen.

"Fire!" he cried, and shot his arquebuse into the air. The report was followed by Bloom's musket.

The warriors fell back, amazed at the strange noise. The boy thought that it would be received on shipboard as a token of danger. He knew that help would come to them. The only question was whether it would come in time.

They turned to try flight to the boat. It would mean being a little nearer to their friends. The Indians were too many for them, while their better acquaintance with the forest stood them then in good stead. Before Giles and his companion had taken a half dozen strides they were surrounded. Lassoes were thrown around their necks. They were prisoners.

They were dragged along over the roots of trees, over rocks and moss, through thorns and bogs, for what seemed hours of flight. Giles understood the purpose, — to bring them beyond the reach of assistance. His sinking heart admitted that there was every probability of success. How could Hudson and his men trace them through this trackless forest?

"All is lost!" gasped Bloom, when they paused at length.

"Keep up hope," Giles answered. But he had little hope himself.

A bark village dotted the valley upon which they had descended. The captives were led to a wigwam which was stationed in the centre, so that it was observable from every point of the compass. They were thrust inside, falling over, half dead with fatigue, upon the mats with which the shelter was lined.

"If I had a drop of water," said Bloom, "I think I should be willing to die. My thirst is greater than my fear."

"And your thirst, at least, can be allayed," replied Giles. For the mat which hung across one of the two entrances was thrust aside. A dish of water and another of parched ground corn were set down near them by a stooping figure, dim in the twilight. In another instant they were left alone once more.

"Cheer up," said Giles. "You see they don't mean to torture us."

He had been thinking, during that weary journey, of some of Captain Smith's stories, repeated by Juet, regarding the Virginian natives, and of other dreadful tales brought home by the French fur-traders from Canada, to which he had often listened in the old days in Paris.

Bloom drank heavily. He even ate a handful of the strange food. He announced that it heartened him. "Come, Valentine," he added, "take what ease you can."

Giles felt that this was the part of common sense. He made a good meal. Afterwards he lay down beside his comrade, alert for a move from their captors.

"Whatever they do," he mused, "will be done quickly, for fear of pursuit."

And some one again thrust aside the mat which hung at the door of the tent.

CHAPTER XXII

WHAT HAPPENED ON HUDSON'S RIVER

THE prisoners sprang to their feet. A warrior, hideous in the dashes of color upon his cheeks, was beckoning to them.

"Are we going to our trial?" said Bloom, turning his pale face towards Giles.

"I am afraid we can scarcely expect justice. More likely it will be swift execution. Be brave, man. If God wills that we die, we can but die like heroes."

Giles's poor Dutch put a barrier between them at this moment, when he ardently longed to be a support to his fellow-captive.

They stepped outside the wigwam. "Did you see Winona anywhere?" Bloom hurriedly inquired.

"Not in the attack. But naturally there would have been no women present there. I will look again now. She is our sole earthly reliance."

They were led to the council-house, a larger building than that in which they had been confined, but of the same hasty construction which sufficed for these nomadic tribes. A fire of piled logs burned beneath the hole in the apex of the great tent, through which one could watch the tree-tops and the stars. By the glow it could be seen that the room was half filled with men, lying on their backs or leaning on one arm, all smoking long pipes and surrounding the chief. As the captives were led to the great man's presence, Giles cast a last glance here and there, seeking Winona. Yes, she stood back of her husband, gazing directly at him. Her eyes were blazing with anger. They did not soften when they met his own.

Now he surrendered all hope. He felt that her presence was intentional, — that she was to be their accuser.

The chief shot a penetrating glance at Bloom. He said a few words to the woman. She stepped forward, fell into an attitude of abject humility at his feet, and poured forth a torrent of words; entreaty, fury, scorn, accusation, seemed mingled in their flow.

"Do you think she is pleading for our lives?" Bloom murmured.

Giles shook his head. He could not tell him that he imagined she was asking for their death. When Winona ceased, and rose to her feet, a man advanced, then another and another. The young chieftain came last. Each spoke rapidly and at length. Each waved a hand towards their prisoners. Each showed in his wrathful manner that what he said boded them no good.

Finally the chief stood up. He motioned to several bystanders, who came forward. Giles was thrown suddenly upon his back. Some one stooped at his feet, binding them together. Some one else pressed a hand upon his forehead. His arms were tied loosely together over his breast. Bloom watched this performance with considerable curiosity.

" Why are they doing that to you, I wonder," he said, " and not to me ? "

As he spoke the chief's son stepped back of him. He bore a heavy club. He had been chosen to avenge the insult that this white man had offered to his father.

Giles gave a warning cry. It was too late. The little brave raised the murderous weapon. With a lightning-like swiftness it fell and crashed upon Bloom's uncovered head. He dropped lifeless to the floor.

Giles waited in momentary expectation of the same fate. He said an earnest prayer.

He thought of Jan, of Meg, and of Annemie. He heard loud discussion beside him and looked up. A group surrounded the chief, Winona among them. As he guessed, they were disputing his future, and whether it should be life or death. A respite was the utmost that the woman could gain. He was seized by his hands and feet and carried back to the wigwam. There he was thrown upon the ground and left alone again.

Hours dragged by, and the sounds outside all died away. The fire from the council-house, which Giles watched dully through the one clear opening to his hut, burned into ashes, and it was dark. He began cautiously to work his hands up and down in their soft leather thongs. Could he free himself? And if he could, would it be of any avail? The prison was closely watched; the woods were well known to his captors, and all unknown to him.

The moon rose, and a long, pale ray fell athwart the entrance to the tent to the spot where Giles was lying. He thought, as it crept towards him, that he never should see the moon rise again: this, he firmly believed, was his last night on earth. Now a shadow crossed the streak of light. A dark form glided noiselessly into the wigwam. A knife glittered in one outstretched hand. Giles shut his eyes, breathing a petition that the end might be sure and speedy, and that he might show no cowardice. He heard the light step glide over the mats to his side. He felt the pause. The gaze bent upon him seemed to burn through his closed eyelids. The cold touch of the knife fell against his folded hands where they were tied upon his breast. He thought it was directed towards his heart. He waited, in the perfect stillness, for the fatal stroke.

There was a slashing movement. The bands about his wrists were severed. Giles's eyes flew open. The figure was kneeling by his feet. The thongs there, too, were cut.

It was Winona. In her black hair, gathered at her neck, there were copper ornaments that glittered in the moonlight. She wore a long skin cloak, richly embroidered in quills and fantastic color designs. Her face was strained, as if listening for a sound. She touched her lip lightly with one finger, and then held it up before her in a warning attitude. Giles could interpret the gesture to mean " Caution ! "

He sprang upright. She led the way, he

creeping after her. The irregular lines of wigwams were bathed in the moonlight. Before his prison lay an Indian guard. He breathed heavily as they stepped timidly past him. Giles glanced questioningly at the woman, wondering if, as seemed probable, she had drugged the watcher. She flew like a bird across the open space. He followed more clumsily, yet with the prudent secrecy learned in his adventurous boyhood. They reached the quiet woods in safety. The moonlight filtered through the tree-tops, showing them dimly the path to go. Winona glided on in advance, a shadow guide. She knew their course where Giles saw nothing to mark it. She pushed between the tree-trunks, and over rotting logs. She threaded her path through the stifling underbrush, holding back the trailing vines that he might follow her. They went on thus for hours. Gray dawn was creeping over the blackness in the eastern sky when Winona reached back, caught Giles by the hand, and showed him a little stream, over which they made a flying leap together. She pulled him after her down a sharp incline. They wound their course through the trees.

The beach lay before them. The Half

Moon swung at anchor out in the river. Giles stifled an exclamation: here was safety once more. Winona pointed towards the boat he and poor Bloom had left there ten hours before.

Then she turned back to the woods. Her self-imposed duty was performed. He was prepared with the means of escape to his friends. Giles felt at his wits' end for a way of expressing his gratitude, when they had not a word in common. He ran after her, fell on one knee, and, grasping the border of her gay, embroidered cloak, raised it to his lips. The act of homage was natural to one reared in the courtly days of Elizabeth, and in the Paris of Henry of Navarre: it was a revelation to the savage woman, used to the treatment accorded a squaw, — that is, all the cruelty and the drudgery which a human being could undergo. She looked down upon the boy with a lovely expression of motherly tenderness on her withered, ugly face. She stooped over Giles's bent head and flung something about his neck. When he stood up and looked about him, she had vanished.

He took her gift in one hand to examine it. It was a bit of soft stone pierced to hang on a strip of leather like a cord, and carved in the rude semblance of a tortoise. Although Giles could not guess its full significance, — that it was the emblem of Winona's people, her totem, — he foresaw its importance in future intercourse with the Indians of her own clan. He appreciated that the tremendous service of his escape was crowned by this act.

He pushed off in the boat, rowing rapidly to the Half Moon's side. He expected, of course, the watch. He had not thought the first person he should see would be Jan, answering his call, and peering down at him doubtfully from the deck.

"It seems too good to be true," he cried, when he held his friend by both hands, and was gazing rapturously into his face. "I have lurked about here all night, watching the shore, and wondering what had become of you. Where is Bloom?"

Giles was soon surrounded by a group of men equally curious to hear his own adventures and to learn their comrade's fate. He saw their dissatisfaction. The crew generally would have cared very little had he never returned to the ship. Bloom, on the contrary, had been a leader among them. Their laments for him were not only loud but also indignant.

"They think I could have saved his life as well as my own," said Giles to Jan.

The latter could not deny that he had listened to murmurs to that effect. When the shots were heard from the ship, a party had been sent out by Hudson. They made a thorough search for the two, without avail, and were obliged to return to the Half Moon, leaving the boat on a slender chance of an escape which might require it to follow them. There had been a sorrowful night between Giles's disappearance and his return.

Nothing more was seen of the Algonquins. The voyagers weighed anchor and sailed on up the river. From time to time, as they passed the banks dropping into the water, a canoe shot out from the forest ridges, making its way to the vessel. Its occupants were always perplexed and excited by the white men's peculiar dress, and tongue, and manners. They exchanged a few trifling gifts, but did not stop to parley with such visitors. Hudson was too feverishly anxious to pursue his investigations: his men saw that their welfare was bound up with his. They were all consumed by the one desire to hasten on and learn the worst — or best.

Not many miles had been passed before

they came in upon what looked like a lake. Hudson's eyes glowed. His cheeks flushed with excitement. He could not restrain the quiver in his tone.

"I believe we are on the right road, Juet," he said to his mate.

"It looks like it," Juet answered quietly.

Truly it did, for a time. But the river narrowed again, as it had widened. They sailed between its evergreen banks, day by day, looking, with hopes that died hard, for other signs that this was Hudson's arm of the sea, and not a river shallower as they ascended it.

"The anchor is going overboard," Giles exclaimed, springing up at the well-known rattle of the chain. "What can be the reason? Do you suppose that we are to make land explorations?"

"Perhaps, in one of the boats," suggested Jan. "If so, I mean to apply for a place."

"And I."

"Oh, no, Giles. Stay on the ship this time!"

Giles gave a derisive laugh at the notion. He understood Jan's uneasiness concerning his treatment from the men. He had no intention of giving in to it, to this extent.

He found that the captain had issued orders for a boat's crew to start at once upon a further search. The expedition would be absent several days,—"as long as necessary," said Hudson, looking depressed and fretted. He was selecting the men. His glance fell upon Giles.

"And Valentine," he added.

Jan pushed forward. "May I be of the party, captain?" he asked.

"No, lad, there is no room for more."

Jan opened his mouth to protest. Giles dragged him away.

"What accusation can you bring?" he demanded. "You have nothing at all except surmises, that no one would listen to. We can't harass the captain. He looks as if he were taking a last desperate chance."

For his part, Giles felt quite capable of looking after himself. He promised Jan to do nothing foolhardy, nor ever to trust himself alone with any one or two of the others, for there was likely to be safety in numbers. Nor would his enemies forget that they must report to the captain at the end of the cruise.

They bade each other good-by, these two friends, with more show of feeling than was usual between them. Giles called back cheery last words. Jan watched the bark wistfully out of sight.

It was a week later that he slid down from his perch at the lookout, and saluted Henry Hudson.

"The boat, sir!" he said.

"Art sure?" Hudson's worn face lighted. The old look, as if in expectation of good news, came into his eyes. "I have thought so oft that I saw it, and have been sore deceived."

Jan was sure that no one had watched for that boat with such anxious gaze as his. "They are our men, sir," he said positively.

Hudson stood buried in reverie. He tugged at his beard, his abstracted sight fastened upon the deck. Jan cast a sympathetic glance at him, and climbed aloft again. The commander was startled from his reflections by a sharp cry.

"What is 't, Verrooy?" he called.

Again Jan dropped down the mast, and made his way to Hudson's side. He forgot to remove his cap. He buried his face in his hands.

"They are our men?" exclaimed Hudson.

"They are our men, sir, and they are but four."

Five had gone out from the Half Moon. The boat neared the ship. Its crew crowded to the bow to see the approach, Jan foremost. His worst fears were fulfilled. Giles was not with the rest. To do Hudson justice, his first query, hallooed across the water, was not of what the explorers had found. He set aside his fondest ambition, and he asked: —

"Where is young Valentine?"

It was one of the men who inquired, "What luck, lads?"

The coxswain answered the double question at once. He looked over his shoulder as they grazed the ship's side, and said: —

"We found shallower water and a narrower stream. The English boy wandered away from us in the forest. We searched, but could find no trace of him."

CHAPTER XXIII

WINONA'S TOTEM

MEANWHILE what had happened to Giles?

He made the best of the others' surly companionship. He thoroughly enjoyed the trip's surprises and adventures day after day. They rowed by turn during the shortening hours of light. At night they camped upon the shore, and ate and slept about the fire with one of their number mounted guard.

The men kept together, appearing to scorn him as an outsider thrust upon them. Often they tried to provoke a quarrel by taunts in regard to the death of Bloom. Much of their talk Giles did not understand; much more of it he pretended not to hear; or it was always a safe method of averting an outbreak to shake his head, and ask some stupid question wide of the mark, taking refuge in his notoriously bad Dutch. He restrained the anger it would have been childish to show when so completely in the power of his enemies. Their undisguised malice towards him had this good effect, that it kept Jan's warnings before his mind.

Yet the boy found it a pleasant life. The country was most beautiful. Now and then a tree or a bush blazed out in early autumn coloring. A long range of mountains against the western sky had come, from a dim outline, as they ascended the stream, to assume boldly impressive forms. Looking back at them, the lower hills bore a fantastic resemblance to a giant lying at rest, his knees drawn up, the profile of his face showing sharply against the intense blue of the American heavens. Giles pointed out this Old Man of the Mountains to his companions. They grunted sulkily at his amusement. None of them knew that the Indians in the region of the Kaatskills — for so the Dutch afterwards called these hills — had already noticed and named this singular formation.

Giles wandered about by himself, at night and at morning, when the boat was beached, although he never strayed far from his comrades. These were delightful strolls, rich in treasure trove; new birds and beasts and plants surrounded him. He seldom encountered a native; but if he did, he found that the owner of the soil was more alarmed than the intruder. He grew to love this fair, wild land with a devotion which was far beyond what his longing had been to visit it when he had little idea what it held. He built many air-castles in that time of quiet roaming along the banks of the river, and all their foundations were laid in America.

They came to tributaries which the men wished to explore. Hessel, the man in command of the expedition, refused to allow this, saying very justly that it was growing late in the season, Hudson awaited them impatiently, and they must keep strictly to their errand, — that of learning the capacity of the stream along which they came.

"It is easy to see the end," one of the others remarked finally, with an evil grin. "It will not require much more breaking of our backs at the oar to return with the tidings that this is no royal road to Asia."

"That is true," answered Hessel from his seat at the rudder. "I am beginning to think we might better turn about. The river — for river it assuredly is — grows less navigable for an ocean ship. It is useless to hope for a change."

He pointed the boat towards an island of no great extent lying in the stream. "We might seek a night's lodging here," he announced.

They made their preparations for a meal, Giles roving about in dreary thought of what their message would mean to Henry Hudson. One of the men took his arquebuse and went away into the woods in quest of game. Another was cleaning some fish, for which they cast a line from the boat. To Giles's surprise, when he came to notice it, he observed that the sun was an hour high. They did not usually encamp before twilight. He asked permission of Hessel to walk along the island and look around him. The man nodded, in his boorish fashion, saying nothing. Giles set out in the opposite direction from the sportsman.

He stopped to examine so much that was curious or delightful, he gathered so many flowers and experimented upon so many fruits and berries, that it was only when these last failed to satisfy a hearty appetite, increased by a day of hard work in the open air, that he realized how long he had been away from the others.

He had gone, unconsciously, inland. It was only a few minutes' walk to the boat upon the beach. He sought the river hurriedly, incited not at all by alarm, but by the pangs of hunger. He came out upon the pebbly shore by the blasted oak which he had noticed when he left the water, and had selected for a landmark.

The boat was gone.

Giles stood, struck motionless with astonishment, and looked in every direction. He could not be mistaken in the place. Here was the old tree; there the seat that its roots made, and the flat rock like a footstool. Not ten yards away the boat had been drawn upon the strand. Yes, — he darted forward, — there were the scales and the heads of the fish Tenbroeck had been preparing for their supper. He was left alone.

He strained his eyes till the eyeballs ached. Away to the southward, perhaps a mile from him, — not more, — was the image of a boat. As he became accustomed to the dim light, he saw the regular rise and fall of flashing oars. They were going to the Half Moon. It was no error, no cheat of apprehension: that was the boat, those were his comrades, and they had willfully deserted him.

That night in the wilderness, far from his fellows, was one of the most memorable in Giles's history. Yet nothing happened while he sat, hungry and stiff with fatigue, over the fire he made, and heard the shrill cry of a wolf in the hills across the river, or the light tread of a wildcat on the island, attracted by the glow and warmth, peeping out at the boy from among the trees.

At daybreak Giles's ear caught another sound that brought him to his feet, musket in hand. It was the harsh clatter of a boat drawn across the pebbles. Had the crew repented? Were they returned for him? Or, which was more probable, had they come back with the reflection that dead men are the only ones who tell no tales? Had they become convinced that it was safer to take his life at once than leave him even thus, — a prisoner on a little island, miles away from Jan, Hudson, and Juet, his three friends in this whole western world?

That thought recalled to his mind one other friend, — Winona. He pulled mechanically at the charm about his neck. He was holding it in his palm as he advanced in the direction of that significant noise. A bark canoe swung to and fro on the water. An Indian was stepping jauntily ashore. He fell back, uttering a low cry at the sight of the pale-faced stranger.

An inspiration came to Giles. He sprang forward to meet the man, holding out the stone. The native's glance fell on it. He gave another scream.

"Winona," said Giles.

He pointed down the river. He gesticulated rapidly, describing the squaw in her dress and walk. The Indian followed his movements with wide-eyed alertness.

When Giles's wordless story was told, it was the other's turn. He took a step forward, falling on his face before the boy. Then he raised himself to his proud, full stature, saying some sentences at which Giles shook his head. The man resorted once more to motions. He asked if Winona's charge were hungry, and was answered decidedly in pantomime. He reached into his canoe, brought out a supply of jerked meat and of ripe berries, and laid all on the flat rock at their feet. Giles ate heartily, delighted that this part of his need could be so readily supplied. Yet he had been in no present danger of starvation if left to himself. He was armed, and the wild things of water and wood were not so wonted to the fear of capture as to be difficult to lure. The imperative demand was for some method of arriving at the Half

Moon before she should sail away. How could he make this man understand his want, or bring him to supply it?

In the night watches he had reflected ruefully upon his love for the wilderness, when the likelihood was that the home he had wished for should be his for the remainder of his life. A solitary existence, thousands of leagues from his kindred, with not one white face to look into his own, was no fulfillment of his desire. He grew wild with excitement as he thought now what falsehood of his death the returning party might tell; of Hudson's sympathy with Jan's futile grief; of the homeward voyage to France; of Meg, of Annemie.

He ran to the canoe and waved his hand to the south. He touched his breast and the boat's bow, and stretched out his hand again. The man indicated that he understood. Giles doubted, for the Indian took a place, too, in the little craft, after settling him carefully in it. Perhaps it was better so, although he had small notion how it would all end, while they sped on over the calm expanse of the river. Certainly he could not have managed the canoe himself. He marveled at the owner's skill.

They traveled throughout the day, keeping to the south. At nightfall they camped upon the shore in silent sociability. "If Jan could only see me now!" thought Giles.

When he awakened, another savage had joined them. His first acquaintance motioned for a sight of the mystic stone. He was given into the care of the new-comer, who showed the same awe for him when he had witnessed what he wore around his neck. The following morning the like ceremony was gone through with by another Indian. In each case his former guide left him to the last man, and went back up the river alone. Giles was growing faint with uncertainty as he neared the familiar portion of the stream where he had quitted the Half Moon. Suppose he were too late? He had come across no trace of the ship's boat. Suppose Hudson had already weighed anchor and was gone?

He sat bent forward in the tottlish bark, his eyes riveted upon the windings of the river. A shout broke from his lips. His conductor looked around inquisitively. Giles was waving his cap above his head. He had spied the sail of the Half Moon!

A little later Hessel, walking up and down the deck, stared aghast at the head of the young Englishman suddenly appearing over the side!

"There's a rope dangling," said the boy coolly, pulling himself to a sitting posture; "but I want help in drawing my guide aboard. How are you, officer? You see I followed you."

Even Jan did not hear the full tale of that week's occurrences until after they had left the ship. Giles received silently the captain's rebuke for carelessness in wandering away from the others. He treated those who deserted him precisely as usual, and only appeared to be desirous to reward his faithful Indian, by whom he sent many little gifts to the others who had assisted his flight. He was none too soon in reaching the vessel. Hudson was thoroughly disheartened. All he asked now was to get to port before winter.

The homeward journey was sad. There were many discussions of their route and of other passages.

"I shall not give up yet," said the captain, "for there must be at all events a way to the extreme northwest. Some day I shall seek that out."

"And then will you send for us?" demanded Jan.

"I will bear thee in mind, my lad. Mine own boy has the promise of sailing with his father in another twelvemonth or so. I must not carry all young heads, though I grant thee they have gone well wi' me this voyage."

The youths were obliged to place what faith they could in this partial promise. On their way up the Channel they put in at Dartmouth. Here, to the consternation of them all, the vessel was seized by the authorities. The act was justified solely by the jealousy the English felt for the Dutch. They were determined to keep the service of so eminent a mariner from their neighbors. They finally sent on the Half Moon to Amsterdam, but forbade Hudson to accompany her.

"You will not forget us, sir?" begged Giles at their parting.

"Ay, mayhap we shall sail together again. Such loyalty to a disappointed old seaman should surely be recompensed."

And that was the most he would say.

The first hour at home — at the nearest approach to a home these boys had known in three years' time — was the reward for whatever ill they had suffered in their journey. Meg sprang into her brother's arms. Mme. Chapelain was sweet and good as ever. Her husband and the old nurse were profuse in wondering admiration over all they had endured and seen. Giles told Annemie that he could not tell whether she were glad to see him or not. " Though you welcomed Jan right heartily," he added.

Annemie drooped her pretty head over her embroidery frame, shaking away her curls to steal a modest glance at him.

" You are so changed," she expostulated. " You have grown so tall and manly, and not like the boy I used to know. I feel it afresh each time I see you after a season of absence. I have to begin all over again in the acquaintance."

Giles stared reflectively at his figure in the mirror opposite to him. There was indeed a difference there from the little fellow who long ago used to live at the Grange near Richmond. He regarded his broad shoulders, his rich wavy hair, his bright face touched with the shade of manhood, his stalwart form.

" Jan is of another sort," he said ; " slight, where I am big-framed, and supple and light, where I, maybe, am clumsy. But he, too, has changed, Annemie."

" Ah, but Jan, man or boy, is my brother."

"Annemie,"—he wheeled about from his contemplation of the glass,—"did you like the boy Giles better?"

Her head fell still lower over the work from which her fingers dropped. Her voice sank almost to a whisper.

"On the contrary," she said, "I think I prefer the man."

CHAPTER XXIV

THE VICTIM OF RAVAILLAC

"You have come to Paris at a gala time," said Mme. Chapelain to the returned sailors. "All is expectation of the coronation of Marie upon the 13th of May."

"Why is she to be crowned?" demanded her Dutch nephew bluntly. "I can't understand the ceremony."

His uncle smiled shrewdly. "Others than you are puzzled. By most persons it is deemed the weak fancy of a vain woman. Yet others think she has the right of it. The king was divorced to marry her. It is not beyond imagination that he should try to set her aside in her turn. She has the excuse now that she is to act as regent during Henry's expedition against Cleves. At all events his Majesty makes no secret of his dislike to the whole affair."

. Jan was soon to witness this dislike. On the following day he was sent by his uncle with some unimportant message to the arsenal to the great Sully himself. M. Chapelain had devised the errand; he urged his relative to give the master-general of the ordnance a hint of his recent voyage and the wonders he had seen.

"Such tales never do any mischief," was his comment. "Sometimes they do good. Of all men, Sully is in the way to advance you in your career should he take an interest in you. Of course before this we could not presume to interfere with Prince Maurice's plans for you. But now that you have once sailed under the flag of Holland, as he arranged, I see no reason why France should not send you both out to some lucrative post in Acadia."

Jan secretly thought that Giles and he would prefer explorations with poor, unfortunate Hudson, to money-making under some dissolute noble at a trading-post. However, he said nothing, and dutifully repaired to the arsenal.

After the trumped-up business was arranged, he lingered to answer the questions asked in regard to the discoveries made in America. A door opened behind them. A gentleman entered unannounced. Sully sprang up, and, after a deep obeisance, would have dragged forward a low chair — one made expressly for this visitor — had not Jan been too quick for him. He pulled the seat into place and respectfully moved back. He had often seen that face in the streets of Paris since the night when he first encountered it, masked, in the forest of D'Entrague. The new-comer was Henry of Navarre.

The monarch nodded easily to both. He paid no heed to the young fellow. He evidently thought him a secretary. He burst at once into his grievance.

"Oh, my friend," he said, tapping his spectacle-case with his finger tip, "I hate this coronation! I cannot put my feeling into words, and yet my heart foretells some disaster."

He started up and clapped his hands against his sides. "I shall die in this town! I shall never leave it. They will kill me, for they have no remedy save my death. That coronation will be the cause!"

"Sire, what do you mean?" demanded Sully.

In his surprise he, too, had forgotten Jan. The boy did not know what to do. It seemed the height of insolence to move at such a moment, and call attention to himself. He stood still in his corner. He could not avoid hearing every syllable that was uttered.

"To tell you the whole truth," said Henry abruptly, "I have been told that I should be killed on the first grand occasion; that I shall die in a coach. This is what causes my fear."

"I never heard this before," Sully answered. "It explains what has often roused my wonder: that your Majesty would cry out if forced to enter a carriage, and yet prove fearless, almost to foolhardiness, among cannon, pikes, and swords. Why should you submit yourself to such terrors? Why not leave town to-morrow? The coronation could proceed without you."

The king shook his head. "That would never do," he said shortly.

"Then postpone the affair. Meanwhile, for yourself, sire, you need neither reënter Paris nor step into a coach. Shall I send to Notre Dame and to St. Denis, and stop the workmen? I will do so if you think it best."

"I should be glad," rejoined Henry. "I have my doubts of the queen. Her heart is set on this ceremony."

"She may say what she will," Sully replied

curtly. "She cannot insist if you tell her what you have just now told me."

He turned to touch the bell. He started as he saw Jan, and recalled his presence with a shock. Henry followed the direction of his glance. Both men stepped one pace towards the boy. Jan advanced and bent till the plumed hat in his hand swept the floor.

"Sire, I have proven my discretion," said he, "and my loyalty before this, — the one in a wayside tavern, the other in the D'Entrague wood."

The friendly old monarch frowned, looked at him closely, then laughed, with a somewhat foolish side glance at Sully. "Well spoken," he said. "We have met before, in one of my insane pranks, when he rescued me from D'Entrague, who would fain make a royal capture. How comes the youngster here?"

"He is a nephew of M. Chapelain. He has been voyaging in the western world with Henry Hudson, the Englishman. He brings strange narratives of wild adventure."

"In which he bore an honorable part, no doubt," said the king.

The servant entered and Jan was dismissed.

Apparently Marie de Medicis would not listen to her husband's apprehensions of evil.

The coronation took place on the appointed day. Sully was too ill to appear. The ceremony was performed by the Cardinal de Joyeuse, who had become a priest in his grief at the death of his wife. Naturally Jan was peculiarly interested in all that occurred. He outdid even Giles in his recklessness and in the points for sight-seeing which he managed to secure. The king was particularly cheerful during most of the day. It was told, however, from one to another that at the height of the magnificent service he suddenly shivered and murmured to a friend who stood next to him : —

"How would all this appear if it were the last day, and the Judge were to show himself?"

When Jan returned to his uncle's apartment that night, he wondered if Henry could be more relieved than he, that the day was safely passed, and no mischief had been done.

On the following morning he went back to the Louvre. He hung about, listening to what was said by those who came and went. He was still tormented by an uncertain fear that wakened with him in the morning, and he wished to see the king for himself, to make sure that his predictions were not likely to be fulfilled.

A carriage drove up at the foot of the steps. After what he had said, could his Majesty intend to enter it? It must be so, for the bystanders began to look out for him, murmuring to each other that there was to be a royal visit to Sully, who was still confined to his room at the arsenal.

By and by Henry appeared at the head of the stairs. Jan saw him look back to kiss his hand to the queen, who was watching him.

"Adieu!" he called; "Adieu! I shall only go and come. I shall return instantly."

At the coach door he dismissed his captain of the guard. "We need no one," he said.

His eyes fell upon Jan's face in the crowd. Perhaps the youth's harassed expression brought back to his mind that conversation with the Duke of Sully. Henry smiled sadly at Jan. Then he took his place in the coach.

Jan kept pace with it as it moved away. By the king's side was one noble, and two were opposite to him. Wings projected from each door. In these sat two more gentlemen. They came to the Croix du Tiroir. Jan, from the roadway, heard some one ask his Majesty where he wished to go.

"To St. Innocent," he answered; "near the end of the Rue St. Honoré."

The horses broke into a brisk trot. Jan could not, by his utmost endeavor, keep up with them. Presently, however, a heavy wagon came in the way of the carriage. It was obliged to go more slowly. Jan thus recovered his lost ground. They were passing the iron-mongers' shops. They came to one whose sign was a crowned heart, pierced through with an arrow. From this spot a man sprang out. The coach was between him and Jan, who still caught a glimpse of the burly form as it stepped up on the wheel.

Henry had his left arm raised. His hand was on the shoulder of M. de Montbazon. He was leaning against M. d'Epernon, who sat beside him and to whom he was speaking. The murderer struck twice at him with the short knife he held. One blow glanced away. The other went home. It pierced the side of the king, who gave a cry, —

"I am wounded."

There was a general exclamation. "What is it, sire?"

"Nothing," he answered. That was the last word he spoke.

The coach came to a halt. Some of its

occupants sprang out after the assassin. Jan had already made one leap across the street. He had the man tightly pinioned in his own strong arms, but he was glad to turn over his captive that he might follow the coach. M. d'Epernon had thrown his cloak over the dying king. The carriage was directed towards the Louvre. When the foot of the steps was reached wine was poured down Henry's throat. He opened his eyes, but closed them again. So he was carried into the palace.

Rumors floated about the place of that death-bed and its incidents. One of his councilors laid the cross of his order upon Henry's mouth. While the physician stood by, weeping, and the surgeons were about to examine the wound, he gave a sigh, and all was over.

Those waiting outside heard that the Chancellor Sillery ran into the presence of the queen. She had been told of her husband's wound. She exclaimed at sight of him, —

"Alas, the king is dead!"

To this Sillery replied, in a speech that has become one of the bywords of history, —

"Madame, the King of France never dies."

There was felt to be danger that this murder might be part of a Spanish plot. Jan had the forethought to hurry to Sully without delay. He found that old soldier stretched upon a couch, but he sprang upright, his illness forgotten, at the awful news.

"Ring," he said to Jan, "and give my orders for me. Forty horsemen at once, and we will return to the Louvre."

Jan was among the band when, on their return, they were met by the Duke of Guise. He stopped Sully to tell him that Henry was dead.

"Sir," was the answer, "if your duty you vowed to the king is as strong in you as it should be in all good Frenchmen, swear to show the same allegiance to his son; to shed your blood to avenge this death."

"I do not need to be thus advised," said Guise. "I am forcing others to take the oath."

Sully was not yet certain of what was to follow. He proceeded to shut himself into the Bastile, collected provision from the marketmen, and sent word to his son-in-law to bring six thousand Swiss to Paris.

Before this Jan had returned to his friends. They were filled with consternation at what he had to tell them. It was speedily shown that the crown was in no peril. Ravaillac, the assassin, had no accomplices. Homage was paid to King Louis Thirteenth, who was only eight years old. Sully went to the Louvre to see the child and his mother. He was presented to his new sovereign by Marie, under the title of one of his father's most faithful servants. The following day she went with her son to the Parliament, and was confirmed in her regency.

So Henry Fourth died and Louis Thirteenth was king. Often after this our youths saw the royal family, and noticed the pretty face of the little Henrietta Maria. When they were nearing middle age they sometimes spoke together of those days in Paris, and of the sweet little girl who seemed meant to trip through life as gayly as she trod the rooms of the Tuileries. Yet she was to shed many tears in her time, and know poverty and danger and distress. She was the daughter and the sister, the wife and the mother, of a king. She was to live to wed the "Baby Charles" of England, and troubles were to fall thickly upon her there. All this was hidden in the future. When it came to pass, Giles and Jan were not only growing old and gray, but among far other sights and surroundings than those of beautiful France.

CHAPTER XXV

THE NORTHWEST PASSAGE

"HERE is good news, Giles," said his friend one morning. "A letter has arrived from Captain Hudson. Our best hopes are realized."

Giles looked up enchanted. "Is it another voyage of discovery?"

"So he says."

"And he is willing to take us with him?"

"If we are willing to go."

There was such a protest when the letter was read aloud to the Chapelain household that the youths began to think they must send Hudson a refusal of his offer. Mme. Chapelain and the maidens were horrified at the thought of an Arctic exploration, — for this was to be solely a search for the northwest passage, — and pointed out that it might not end as well as the former one had done, by speedy abandonment of the project in favor of the quest along the lower coast. M. Chapelain, alone, stood by the young men.

"They are old enough," he said. "Full-grown fellows of seventeen. They want to see the world. Hudson is a commander among a thousand. Let them go, say I."

"I own that I am homesick for America," was Giles's admission. "I long to see that land again. I hope this journey will give me another visit to its shores, whether we pass beyond them to India, or not. And I do look forward to the day when we all shall make a home there, on the banks of the river that Hudson found."

The womankind of his party did not look allured by this prospect, although Jan added to it his own views for the future. "Will you allow it to stand thus?" he proposed. "May we go over to England, see Sir Robert Carey, lay the case before him, and, if he accepts for Giles, be free to join the captain?"

This compromise was finally agreed upon. Meg and Annemie were secretly proud of their brothers' daring. They could neither bear to stand in its way, nor utterly to give them up to its promptings. A very sorrowful farewell ensued. All were pretty well assured that Giles's old guardian, after surrendering him to the hands of Jan's uncle, would not be likely to interfere in this present plan. The boys themselves understood what risks they were taking. Yet neither of them could guess what was to happen, nor the length of time that was to pass before they should return. Nor could they know that they all were never to meet on earth again.

One April day, at Portsmouth, the friends were met by their old commander. He greeted them cordially, taking them to his lodgings, where they were introduced to his wife and son. Hudson informed them that there was a vexatious delay in shipping sailors for the voyage.

"If ye care to linger in England for a sennight or so, 'tis no matter," he said. "I should not have hastened ye from France, had I any thought these mischances would rise to hinder us in our start."

The boys assured him that they were glad of the opportunity to make a little visit to their old home. Accordingly, they set out for London, after sending word to Sir Robert, appointing a meeting. Both were so confident that the asking his permission was a mere form, that they had not told Hudson of their promise to their sisters.

It proved exactly as they had expected. Carey was only interested in the expedition, envied them the experience, and bade them Godspeed. He had a wife and babies to show his ward, was happily settled down at Richmond, and had only one discomfort in life. He had married into a Puritan family, and their complaints were as excessive against the government as was Sir Robert's private indignation when any one of his Roman Catholic friends was deprived, because of his religion, of one right and another. King James was managing matters with no more tact, to say the least, than that displayed in the first days of his accession.

Sir Robert told them that George Earl was in Scotland. "Prince Henry is another sort than either of you," said the courtier, shaking his head. "I like not his looks. He hath grown tall, — taller than Giles, — but frail and slender as a reed. England bases too many hopes upon that fair lad. I doubt me they may all come to naught."

After a walk to see Master Carr, and one to the Grange, and a talk with the good old friends who still occupied it as his tenants, Giles was ready to start back to Portsmouth. Jan hastened his departure.

"I shall not feel sure that we are to sail," he said, "till we stand on deck and see the vanishing shore behind us. I feel as if we were to be prevented; there is a cloud hanging over me."

He shrugged his shoulders as if to throw it off.

"Odd!" Giles laughed. "I never set out upon anything that promised so well to my fancy. I see everything through a golden glass."

Their captain did not share these rosy hopes. He was full of trouble. There were sailors in plenty at the port. Such men as he desired, strong of character and of body, — those were not to be procured at will.

"I have shipped one old acquaintance," Hudson said. "Do you remember Hessel?"

"Yes," Giles answered, "I remember him very well."

Before the month had passed they had sailed away from land. At the moment that they caught their last glimpse of England, Giles reminded his friend of his foreboding.

"It has come to nothing, you see," he added. "Although I grant you one's inclination would not seek out such fellow-passengers as ours. Were there ever such murderous faces outside a prison?"

"The Half Moon's crew were angels to

them," Jan assented. "Hessel quite shines beside the others. Yet I wish he were anywhere rather than here."

The ship bore steadily away to the northwest. In June they approached the coast of Greenland. As far as the eye could reach fields of ice covered the ocean. The appearance was of a multitude of white islands dotted over the sea. There were broad lanes of water zigzagging about, through which Hudson made a path. The way behind them was closed at once. As far as the horizon nothing could be seen save the floes, some of them miles in extent. There was no landing upon the eastern coast of Greenland. For leagues before them the broken ice intervened.

Their course lay to the south of the island. Here at the east they hoped to find a port. Now icebergs came into sight. Because of the ice-fields there was no keeping out of their way. They were obliged to sail among them, the tall, fantastically shaped peaks looming over the masts, their surfaces chilling the air. It was a fearful experience. Horror was added to horror by rumbling sounds and reports like those from a cannon, when a berg broke into pieces and fell scattering into the sea. Night and day the awful cold, the awful noises continued, while they slowly, carefully picked their way through this frozen world.

One day a boat's crew put out, of course by the captain's permission, but rather against his better judgment, into one of the broader water lanes, on a seal hunt. The fields hereabouts were covered with these animals, some of them sleeping upon the ice, some rolling over and over like puppies at play, some popping their sleek heads above the water, then diving out of sight. Jan went with the men. Each was armed with a club. They scattered in every direction, meaning to creep upon and surprise the seals before they should take fright. They sprang among a group of a dozen beasts, hit right and left, knocking them upon the nose, then dragged them by a rope to the boat. Soon a great number had been killed in this fashion. The boat was obliged to make repeated trips to the ship. It looked like useless slaughter, but the crew understood how needful these skins would be in their further Arctic journey.

After thus going to and fro a half dozen times, the men returned for the last heap piled upon the edge of a floating cake of enormous size. Hudson warned them to be particularly careful.

"Keep your eyes on the ice," said he. "It is moving slowly together. I fear you will be caught."

From the ship they saw the men leap out of the boat. Cracks began to run faster and faster through the ice. The grinding of its sides together, the sharp sound from the splitting mountains, echoed like a bombardment. The ship was hemmed in by enormous hills. Between them the party on the field were espied running back to their boat. A seal suddenly peeped its head out of a crack across which Jan was springing. He started, tripped, and fell. The men before him looked around at the noise. Those behind ran to his assistance. Their loud reproaches for his clumsiness, and the delay it caused, broke in upon the voice of nature. The accident was the means of saving their lives. The foremost had been ready to jump into the boat. Now, before they could reach it, the contracting ice took it between its jaws. There was a hideous crushing movement. It was smashed to atoms, like an eggshell underneath a weight.

"To the ship! to the ship!" arose a call.

There was not an instant to be lost. The hills and hummocks, bearing down upon the bark, not only threatened its destruction, but made approach more uncertain with every second. One by one the men, leaping, climbing, sliding, came into view. They were pulled on deck by their comrades there.

The ice split in front of them as swiftly as it had closed in. A long lane opened out, and dangerous as it was, bordered by toppling bergs and advancing fields, it yet promised present deliverance. They went forward with the utmost caution.

Not long after this, land was seen upon the east, — a point of Greenland near where Hudson had heard of a settlement that existed for several centuries, but was finally wiped out by the plague. He was in hopes that somewhere in the neighborhood he might find natives with whom they could trade, and who could give them information in regard to their route. They effected a landing by means of the ice, that was here immovable, stretching out from the coast for many yards. It was a rather pleasant day, chilly but not cold, with a brilliant sun shining on the rocks and patches of green grass. Hudson directed Giles and Jan to make a search along the shore for Esquimaux. To the boys' surprise, Hessel requested permission to accompany them. He walked along beside them for a time without a word. Then he broke out: —

"I've looked for a chance to talk with you, Valentine, ever since we left England. I want to tell you that I have not forgotten how you behaved to me on the Half Moon."

Giles looked puzzled; partly because he did not altogether understand the Dutchman, and partly because his speech might be taken in two ways.

"How did I behave?" he asked.

"You kept your tongue between your teeth. I suppose Verrooy knows all about it. I can see that Hudson does n't. You had us in your power, and yet you never betrayed what had happened when we left you alone on the river."

"That's all past and done with," said Giles, embarrassed by the praise.

"No; it is not done with. I may have a chance some day to pay you for it. If the opportunity comes, I shan't forget how you stood by me then. Mark my words!"

He spoke with solemnity. Giles quickly turned the subject.

"There are huts!" he exclaimed, hastening his steps. "Ah! there are natives coming to meet us. The captain was right."

They broke into a run.

The dirty, forlorn hovels were constructed of ice and snow. Bearskins hung at the tunnel entrance, and lay upon the floor inside. The squalid people, wrapped in furs, who thronged about them, carried them hospitably forward, chattering ceaselessly in a language of which none of them could understand a word.

"It is a warm welcome, at all events," Jan observed. "We can make that out from their gestures and grins. They want us to visit them."

One man was a sort of leader. He secured all three for his prize, and walked them into his wretched home. An old woman was chewing strips of skin, which, her husband showed his guests, were thus rendered soft and pliable, and made into articles of clothing.

Two lamps burned dimly in the close room. They were of soapstone, scooped out, lined thickly with dried and powdered moss, and half filled with oil. Over these were hung two pots, in which wild duck was stewing. It would have been a savory odor, had it not mingled with the offensive smells of the filthy spot.

The sailors were accustomed to making the

best of things, but they were likewise used to the exquisite cleanliness of shipboard.

"Let us take the man back with us to Hudson," Hessel suggested. "I would rather have him for guest than host." And he seized the Esquimau by the arm.

CHAPTER XXVI

AN ARCTIC WINTER

The native was very willing to accompany them. Several of his friends, who were not included in the invitation, also attached themselves to the party. Hudson was delighted with the prize his explorers brought back with them.

He found that there was little progress to be made between them by signs. He could not understand the man, nor could he be sure that the man understood him.

"We shall have to depend upon making our discoveries for ourselves," he finally announced. "If this fellow knows anything of a passage to the East, we shall not find out from him. I had hoped that some words of a European language — something that we could comprehend — might have been left from the traditions of the old Danish colony."

Harry Hudson was not old enough to share fully in his father's disappointment. He took the most unfeigned pleasure in the stranger's appearance, and was good-naturedly shown the breeches and boots of bearskin, the underclothing of birds' skin, the coat and hood of fox, the seal mittens and stockings. While he was examining and exclaiming in childish curiosity, his elders watched Hudson's expressive face.

"Another blow, where he has had so many!" thought Jan.

They sent away the Esquimau with some trifling trinkets that made him grunt for joy. Without more delay, the order was issued to put out again to sea.

Some days followed, of the life that was beginning to grow monotonous even in its endless hazards. At a snail's pace they stole among towering hills and level patches of glistening ice. The captain kept a man constantly in the rudely constructed crow's-nest aloft. It was muttered among the crew that some sign of the long-expected passage must soon come, or — significantly — it would be too late.

"There is only one end to such an unequal fight between Man and the Frost," said Hessel to Jan. "And some day we shall see that end."

"Well, we all sailed in this expedition with

our eyes wide open," was Jan's answer. "We understood our leader's plans, and what they involved. He has not deceived us."

Hessel shot a sidelong sly glance at him. He opened his lips, as if to say something more, but closed them quickly and went away.

These three from the old Half Moon, with the Half Moon's commander, all recalled that day when the river far to the south was sighted; for, on a bright July morning, there was the same hail from the lookout: —

"Water on the larboard side!"

It was not long before they all could see it: a plain, broad highway, although it was fringed with ice. Henry Hudson clasped his hands in thanksgiving. His eyes swept the vast horizon to a wide stretch of sea. Surely this was the goal of his fondest dreams, — another path to the Indies. It grew in likelihood with each hour, while they advanced through the strait into the bay, both of which were to be called in coming years by his name, as was the river he had found to the south. These Arctic waters were to prove as deceptive as the other.

In these warm months they sailed with comparative freedom across the great gulf, their certainty becoming more assured, when its size was seen, that it was the arm of the sea to lead them through the land.

Alas! they came finally to its borders. They put about; north and south they flew, like an animal in a trap trying all its confines. Each rocky wall proclaimed, "No thoroughfare."

The short summer was going in the search. The strait had led them through its icy gates, but they were now closed. It was idle to look for egress before another year.

"We must winter here in the north," announced the captain. "Our search can be prosecuted in the spring."

The prospect was not bright for any one. The men took it very ill. They said among themselves that the entire voyage had been a failure through Hudson's bungling. On all occasions Giles and Jan stood up for their leader. Had it not been for Hessel's rough championship, they might have fared badly among the crew. The most apparent effect of frequent quarrels on the subject of their misfortunes was that the youths kept more and more with Harry and his father, and left the others to themselves.

For the extremest cold the ship was abandoned, it being the captain's opinion that they would be safer on land than on the vessel, when the ice closed in around it. They found a peculiarly fortunate situation for their temporary home. At the foot of a steep hill on a small island there were massed together several piles of rock, split from the cliff and lying upon the stony beach. Two of these pieces had fallen so as to form a very crude sort of tent some twenty feet across the bottom, and rising to that height at the top. Heaps of stone lay against this at the back. In front, it would be no difficult task to lay a low tunnel entrance for protection and warmth. The rocks could be mortared together with moss and mud. A chimney could be raised by all the hands they had at leisure, during the long daylight of an Arctic summer.

The glare of the sunshine on snow was wearisome; the complaining men brought it forward for another grievance. Yet their groans were redoubled when darkness fell. There were forerunners, first, of the winter. The birds began to leave them, the grass and flowers died, ice formed upon the water, snow squalls were common, the wind howled pitilessly, and the days grew shorter.

The men made themselves clothing of the sealskins, and from the pelt of an occasional fox which they shot. So far no one had seen a bear. Birds were often caught. They used the soft skin, covered with down, for hoods.

Their supply of food was readily procured. The water and land fowl were tame; they shot them in vast quantities, or hunted their nests for eggs. Hudson had supplied his vessel with ammunition and with provision, having this emergency in view. Perhaps, if the men had been in positive danger, they might have clung to their chief in the devotion that such an event excites. They had nothing worse than discomfort to bear, and they did not bear it well. Unfortunately, the captain set all their wrath down to mariners' temper, and was not on his guard against it.

They moved into their land quarters, carrying their valuable possessions from the ship. The autumn twilight fell. Then followed darkness, utter and black. It was night, beyond any night they had ever known. It would have been unbearable, they thought, were it not that the white covering of the snow served to give a dim, reflected light by which they could move about. Even under these conditions they were at a disadvantage; but they were not entirely prisoners.

Giles and Jan were accustomed to going out upon the ice or along the shore on long walks. This was partly for exercise and from restlessness, partly to get out from their crowded room and the companionship of the crew, partly that they might enjoy each other's society. Harry often begged to accompany them. They could not refuse, although his presence prevented some consultations they would have liked to hold.

For things were not going well in the camp. The men got together in groups to converse in scowling whispers. They gave a sullen obedience to their captain's commands. They always stopped talking when he or his son or either of the youths approached.

"Suppose I take Hessel away, on some pretext," Giles suggested, "and try to find out what they are about."

He soon discovered an excuse. Going out for a can of water, he saw, as he stooped to break through the ice, a track upon the snow that drew his closer attention. It was differently marked from the light pat of a fox. It looked a little like the imprint of a child's naked foot. Giles dashed back to the inclosure. He crept through the entrance, thrust back the blankets that hung across the rocky doorway, and touched Jan's prostrate form.

"Do you want to go bear-hunting?" he whispered.

Light as had been his steps and low as was his salutation, a half dozen shaggy heads raised themselves from their slumber-bags, and glared at him through the gloom. Hessel was one of the awakened men. Jan sat up with a joyful start. He sank back, remembering their last conversation, when he caught the Dutchman's glittering eyes.

"Take Hessel," said he. "I cut my hand yesterday, you remember. I could not hold a musket."

Giles was scarcely less disappointed than his friend. What a memory it would be, for the remainder of their lives, if they could kill their first bear together! Yet he saw what Jan's thoughtfulness had grasped at once: this was the opportunity, when opportunities were rare, for an appeal to their only ally among the disaffected men.

Hessel was pleased to go, and was ready in a twinkling. They said nothing of their errand to the others, stealing out by themselves into the dark.

Giles led his companion to the track on the snow. They followed it along the broken ice on the shore to the storehouse the crew had built, like a snow fort, against the rocks. A shout of dismay pealed out from them both. It resounded in the camp. The men came pouring out of their retreat.

"What is wrong?" called Hudson.

Giles pointed in silence. He could not find speech for the catastrophe. The captain hurried up, the men following. The extent of their disaster broke in upon them all at once.

Not one bear, but several had been there while they slept.

There were confused tracks wandering about the spot. Their precious hoards had been dragged out from their hiding-place. Blocks of snow were pitched aside. Stones were rolled hither and thither. Skins were torn away. The food that had been saved to secure their future was eaten, trodden underfoot, mangled, destroyed. There was not enough left for a single day's rations for all those hungry men.

There was no more thought of a secret conference between Giles and Hessel. The crew flew to the tent for their weapons.

Giles and Jan, together after all, ran forward with Hudson and the Dutchman. They were on the track of two bears. They came to an ice hillock, where the animals separated. Hudson and Hessel went to the right. Giles and his crippled comrade, the latter regardless of his wound, took the other direction.

"Hist! there it is," said Jan.

"There are three!" was the quick answer.

One was a cub; one was half grown; the third was an immense fellow, weighing fully one thousand pounds. They were worrying the carcass of a fox that had been shot and skinned the day before.

The boys went across the ice on tiptoe, Jan holding his long knife in his maimed hand. Giles aimed his musket at the largest beast. Its head was turned away; its nose was in the snow against the fox. Jan was slightly in advance. The great bear cocked its ears, wheeled clumsily about, and was on him in another moment.

How it happened neither of them could ever tell. Jan threw himself forward, plunging the dirk into its neck, behind the lower jaw. The blood gushed out in torrents. The bear gave a roar that shook the rocks. The other animals scrambled up, only to follow their leader as it ambled away over the snow. The boys kept hard upon them.

The stream of blood guided where it was impossible to take such strides as their game. The cub fell behind. Giles shot it; food had become a matter of importance. He hurried on, following the trail among the hillocks, eager to be in at the death, or at least to gain some glory by a blow at the larger young one.

A cry aroused him from these thoughts. It was Jan's voice. He was calling aloud for help.

CHAPTER XXVII

MUTINY

Giles's feet felt clogged with lead, yet he ran over the uneven ice with incredible speed, led by the trail of blood no less than by Jan's shouts. The track of the bear became more and more crooked. He could see how it was wavering. He was not surprised to find it presently, lying upon its side, dead. Jan was not here, so Giles sped on.

He came in sight of his friend, who had rashly attacked the third bear. His lame hand had given out. He had wounded the infuriated animal, and a fierce combat was going on. Jan was in sore straits.

He had been thrown on his back. One great paw, planted upon his breast, was crushing out his life. The beast's hot breath blew in his face. He could see the small angry eyes, glowing like coals of fire, close to his own.

The difficulty was to harm the bear without also injuring the boy. Giles surveyed the two in deep perplexity, feeling that he must make an instantaneous decision. He lifted the musket he happily had loaded beside the cub he shot. A sharp report rang out through the foggy air. The puff of smoke cleared away. Giles had chosen well. The bear was hit in the back, — a broad target presented to him while the struggle between man and beast was waging. It was only a flesh wound, though it served its purpose. It attracted Bruin's attention, and turned it upon this new adversary.

Jan scrambled to his feet. He picked up his knife where it had fallen in the mêlée. He sped nimbly towards Giles, putting their foe between them. Giles rapidly reloaded. He shot once more, and missed.

"Your knife! your knife!" screamed Jan, as the brute, head down and growling savagely, plunged awkwardly forward.

Giles pulled out the dirk. He endeavored to imitate his companion's successful blow. His mind was as clear as the senses often become in such seasons of supreme peril.

"Behind the lower jaw and below the ear," he reflected. "That was Jan's stroke, and it was fatal."

He made a swift pass at the spot. What

Jan had done by a mere chance blow he could not deliberately accomplish. He inflicted a deep flesh wound, without striking the artery. One of those paws struck him and knocked him flat upon the snow. Jan fell on the bear. His knife flashed back and forth through the air. His lithe, slender figure moved like a shadow. Giles's sturdier bulk had been overthrown, but Jan was not to be again surprised, as he had been when the bear first turned on him. He kept out of range of those flying paws, the open scarlet mouth, the wicked long white teeth.

By the time his breath came shorter, his blows grew feebler, Giles was up again.

"Load and fire!" panted the young Dutchman. "I can — keep him — busy — a moment — more."

Only a moment, yet it sufficed. Another loud report echoed from the hills. Bruin was weakened by loss of blood and by the energy of these strange antagonists. Giles's shot took effect. The heavy bulk trembled, and lurched from one side to the other. It fell prone upon the snow. A quiver ran through the body. Then all was still.

The boys dragged this mass of flesh and fur — both needed by their party — to the place where Jan's victim was found. Here they met Hudson and Hessel. They had been unsuccessful. The tracks they followed doubled, leading them around to the storehouse. Evidently there were but three bears in the first place. Jan and Giles had shot them all.

The cub was secured, and the enormous white bear was skinned and cut into pieces where it lay. There was food for the present provided in plenty, even for twenty-five men. That number must look for more game, if they were not to know before long what short rations meant.

No bears appeared after this for several weeks. Then one was killed by a man on the watch. Occasionally some one shot a fox. Ammunition was running short, now that they were forced to depend entirely for food on what they hunted. One day Giles and Harry were strolling about on the ice, when the latter thrust one foot into a large opening made by some animal. It was covered by a snow crust, so that neither had noticed the weak spot in that uncertain light.

"It is a seal-hole," Giles said, examining it more closely. "Harry, look about thee. Mayhap we shall find others. If seal are plentiful, we shall not go an hungered, after all."

Harry privately thought that seal meat would be no delicacy. However, he was eager for the sport. "I will do whate'er you say, Master Valentine," he promised.

Giles reflected for an instant. "Run to the camp and bring me two of the Esquimau's spears," he said, "with a few fish-lines as well."

At last some part of their barter with the man in the Greenland village was to prove of use. Harry was back again in an instant. After considerable trouble, Giles fastened the spears to one line. Then they waited beside an air-hole for a seal to appear.

It was not long before they heard a puff; a little shower of spray flew up through a tiny crevice in the crust. Giles plunged his spear like a flash. It hit the seal's neck and drove down into the flesh.

Away went the seal. The spear went with him. The line played out; the spear at its other end flew wildly about the ice; when it reached the hole it lodged across it, and, though jerked to and fro, could go no farther. The seal pulled and strained to no avail. By and by its head appeared at another hole near at hand. The line was loosened. The boys began to wind it around the spear they held. Whenever the entrapped animal came to the surface to breathe, they were on the watch for it. They drew in more and more of the line, until they had the seal secure in a certain hole. Then the blows Giles aimed with his knife took effect. At last they had captured their prize.

Skinning the beast was a tedious and disagreeable piece of work that was divided among the men. The blubber was removed, and stored away for use in lighting and heating the tent. The meat was cut into strips, and also stored, — with infinite precautions nowadays, — nor did Harry disdain a hot seal steak.

All this time neither Giles nor Jan had found opportunity for a talk with Hessel. It was obvious that the man avoided them. It was no less apparent to the friends that something was amiss among the men.

Light began to dawn. At first there was a little flash at midday. It grew more and more to the glow of an early dawn. Then, the following day, the sun appeared a little higher above the horizon, and a little higher still. The long day had begun. The snow melted. Streams rushed down the cliffs to the bay. The ice became soft and cracked, and the winds carried it about in floes and hills that finally drifted out to sea.

Grass grew green on the slopes. Delicate small plants bloomed into lovely life. Birds came back. There were ducks and geese and gulls for food. The seal basked on the rocks in the sunshine. They spied walruses and narwhals. A white bear crossed the ice one day, but too far away for an attempt at capture.

Hudson began his preparations for departure. Throughout the long winter he had employed his leisure hours by many schemes. A terrible obstacle faced him. The wanton destruction of their storehouse in that one night long ago had ruined his provisions. He set the men to salting and jerking meat, but it was absurd to think of laying in sufficient to last so large a number throughout a further extended voyage. Many a time he bitterly reproached himself that he had removed the stock from the ship. But it had not been at all certain that the vessel, locked in the ice, would ride out the winter. It had appeared to be the part of prudence to take everything necessary with them to land.

The crew, busily employed in the bright sunshine, kept their heads together, muttering what, their lowering faces hinted, boded no good to some one. At last the storm broke.

Hudson called all hands together on board the ship. A boat was plying back and forth between it and the shore, where an impromptu kitchen was built. Every one hastened to the deck. Their leader's views were shrewdly surmised, yet he had taken no one into his confidence. He looked into a semicircle of scowling countenances. Jan and Giles were the only two who responded cheerfully to the invitation for a conference. Harry stood beside his father, whose hand rested upon the boy's shoulder.

"You know already, men," the captain began in Dutch, "why we have come to this land of desolation; what we hope to find before we go back to our homes. Every other consideration must give way to the one of accomplishing our purpose. Now, how may we set about that further exploration? We were provided with what, by strict economy, might have sufficed for food. Since we have lost that supply, we are laying in stores that will keep a dozen men, perhaps, from starvation for " —

He was interrupted by a murmur that rose among the men, and swelled into a roar of protest.

" A dozen men ? " repeated Hessel.

Hudson saw his mistake. He should have introduced his scheme by degrees, and have left the settling of its details to those chiefly concerned. Jan, also, grasped the situation. He stepped forward.

" Captain Hudson," he began in his clear, ringing voice, " I will be the first to volunteer. I will stay behind."

Giles had been listening, with bent brows, to what was half unintelligible to him in the foreign tongue. He did not know at all what Jan meant. He had no idea to what he pledged himself. But he felt certain that his friend's agreement was right and fair. Wherever Jan went he should follow. He strode to the side of the young Dutchman.

" And so will I," he said.

Hudson glanced at the others. Not one moved. Hessel growled protestingly to the lads : —

" What will become of you if you do remain here ? Are you contented never to quit this spot ? "

" Not at all," said Jan loudly. He assumed

a confidence he did not feel. "We shall make our way southward overland. We shall not be unarmed entirely." For he perceived that the rest were thinking, as he was then, of the scanty ammunition. "There are whalers along the coast. There are settlements of the French " —

" And the Spanish," interrupted some one, with a hoarse laugh.

" Yes, and the Spanish, thousands of miles away. Even though we fall in with no white men, we deserve to die if we cannot find a living in that fertile land that Hessel, at least, remembers, no less than Valentine and I. We deserve to die," — his tones pealed out like a trumpet, — " if we are not willing to do this for our captain, and for the common good."

The men looked doggedly at one another, and then towards him. Hessel's features worked nervously.

" I do remember that land," he said meaningly, catching the expression of Jan's speaking eyes. " I would be willing to cast in my lot with you two younkers, but the thing is impossible! A dozen men could not live in such a march without provisions, nor the means of finding more. We have been brought thus far by our commander. I, for one, say that it is his duty to get us out of the fix he has got us into."

"How shall he do it?" asked Jan.

Hessel was their appointed spokesman. No one else said a word. He looked rather taken aback by Jan's blunt query. It was easier to find fault with others' arrangements than to make them for one's self.

Hudson walked towards them. His head was held haughtily aloft. Such plain speech, such criticism of his methods, such symptoms of insubordination, were abhorrent to him. He had deemed it best to let them talk the thing out freely. He thought now that enough had been said.

"I regret," he began scornfully, "that my views do not chime in with those of my crew. Let it be understood that, whether it is your will or no, twelve of us leave this place by ship. Thirteen take the landward path. Twelve go to the east, if the Lord will. Thirteen are sent — and God speed them — back to their homes. And now to your work."

He gave a further rapid order in regard to the labors in which they were all engaged. His manner was that of finally closing the matter. There was to be no appeal.

Not a man stirred.

Hudson raised his eyebrows. A sneer crossed his lips. He repeated his order.

Sixteen men stepped quietly out from the semicircle. Four, moving like parts of a machine, went to their appointed places. Four to one, they seized Hudson, his son, and Giles and Jan. They were prisoners, gagged and bound.

The crew had mutinied. Their long-brooding grievance was ready for instant action, and the action had been taken.

CHAPTER XXVIII

ADRIFT WITH HUDSON

THE prisoners were separated and conveyed to different parts of the ship. It was impossible for them to confer together. They could not devise any concerted scheme for escape or opposition.

It was late in the day, counting by hours, not by sunshine. The men went in squads to their dinner on land, leaving always a full contingent to watch the vessel. Under less serious circumstances, Giles and Jan would have been flattered by the fear manifested that they might effect something, — two against twenty-one. Food and water were brought to them; the bandages across their mouths were removed, and each was asked if he would change his mind, give in to the will of the majority, and abide by its decrees.

No one inquired for little Harry's opinion. His father and the two youths made a firm refusal.

When bedtime came, the same precautions

were adopted. Ten men slept, and ten watched the ship. One patrolled the beach as usual, watching their stores of food.

"Valentine!" whispered a voice close to Giles's ear. "Valentine, are you awake?"

Giles tried to nod his head. The gag was taken from his mouth. Hessel sat down beside him. The other men were detailed, as in this instance, two to a man. Hessel's companion paced back and forth several yards away.

"I want to reason with you," said the Dutchman. "You see how this matter is going. You can't do the captain any good."

"What is to become of him?"

"He and his son will be set adrift in the long boat."

Giles shuddered. "And Verrooy and I?"

"You go with us, or with them."

"You keep to the ship, I suppose?"

"Yes."

Giles rolled over on his side. He could not think of the Dutch equivalent, so he murmured sleepily, "Bon voyage!"

"Do you mean that you hold to Hudson?"

"I mean," — he raised himself on his elbow to explain, — "that I ship with a captain for the entire voyage. I shall go in the boat."

Hessel's brown cheek grew red under the taunt. "What if the captain would leave you behind?"

"It is he, not I, that orders it. My part of the contract is performed."

The Dutchman moved uneasily. "That is what Verrooy said."

"Aha! you have been experimenting with Jan?"

"Yes. He is as obstinate as yourself."

"So I supposed," said Giles calmly, and lay down again.

Hessel lifted the bandage. He stooped over the boy, holding the strip in his hand. "You know what Hudson's fate will be?"

"I know: starvation and torture from thirst, — slow death."

"And you choose it?"

Giles's German was a shade worse than his Dutch. However, he looked steadily into Hessel's remorseful face and quoted Martin Luther's declaration: —

"Here I stand. I can do nothing else. God help me!"

Hessel moved away.

Another meal was brought to them. They were lifted in the arms of the guard and carried to the vessel's rail. The four met for the first time since their arrest. They glanced manfully at one another. Even Harry wore a courageous look. His father was defiant and indignant, but his high demeanor vanished at sight of his champions. They were ungagged and unbound. Hudson found occasion to say to Jan, who stood beside him : —

"Lad, thou shalt not be sacrificed, too! Save thyself."

"Nay, captain," was the serene answer. "Methinks Giles and I are agreed."

"There may be a middle course."

Hudson understood what fate was prepared for him. He saw the boat, its stock of dried fish and its can of water, ready for its occupants. He bore his doom like a hero, although he had stooped to ask mercy for his son. It was refused, and yet he tried once more for these boys.

"Set Verrooy and Valentine ashore," he pleaded aside with Hessel. "Give them some chance for their lives. If they will not ship with you, surely they need not be set adrift with me."

Hessel looked ten years older in the past twenty-four hours.

"I would give my right hand," he answered, "to save Giles Valentine. I have implored the rest to let them wander south if they could; they might reach some bark or a settlement, as Verrooy said. But the others are afraid of that. They want no tales told of what happens here. It must be either the ship or the boat for them. There is no alternative."

He spoke loud enough for the boys to hear. He looked urgently into their faces. Giles exchanged one glance with his friend.

"It is the boat," they said in a breath.

The crew approached the little group. One by one they were conducted into their frail refuge. Hudson seated himself in the stern. Harry clambered into the bow. Giles and Jan picked up their oars. From their manner one might have thought they were departing for a pleasure trip. The rope was cast off. They were left to themselves.

Hudson steered to the northeast. It made small difference in which direction they went, he said. The end was inevitable. Yet mechanically the old captain strove still towards the goal of his ambition, — the strait that should bear him to the open sea, the ocean which carried on its breast the secret of another road to Asia.

The boys plied their oars only to keep the

keel steady. There was no need for exertion. They would require all their strength. Four muskets, a few shot and a little powder lay rolled in a blanket in the bottom of the boat. Hudson surveyed their provision, portioning it out. It might last a fortnight.

"Lads,"—his voice was animated,—"suppose we try the strait in earnest? We might run across a ship outside. Which shall it be? Here we have a shadow of a chance of getting to land; or there are these innumerable islands, if we are minded to cast ourselves away on one of them. On the sea we may have an opportunity of sighting a sail. Choose!"

"Do you vote for the ocean?" asked Giles.

"Aye. I should risk it for myself and my boy."

"I take the risk for myself," said Jan, after a little reflection. "The landing, could we make it, would mayhap only draw out our sufferings. What think'st thou, Giles?"

"The ocean, say I."

They kept on their course towards the strait. They ate and drank, told Harry tales to amuse him, wrapped the boy in his father's cloak, and saw him sleeping peacefully as if he were at home, with his head against Hudson's knee.

They slept, themselves, from sheer exhaustion, when they were utterly worn out. They took turns at the oar. As the long hours went by, the necessity for husbanding their strength became more apparent. They watched and worked, and worked and watched. Harry demanded his share of the labor and responsibility. Hudson said that they could trust him absolutely. The fatal close to this hazardous journey came from the father's faith in his child.

He and his son were rowing the boat. Giles and Jan were asleep. The captain was giving out under the protracted strain. He closed his eyelids over the motion that had become a matter of habit. A wild cry from the boy roused him. The sleepers started up.

Harry's right arm was rigid, he was pale as death. His hand pointed towards the north. They were in the strait, where, even at midsummer, ice is a constant menace to navigation. A berg was bearing down upon them. They were drifting directly in its path.

Giles tore the oars from the boy's lax fingers. It was hopeless to flee from the monster, and yet action — any action — was preferable to sitting still under its approach. Hudson bent to the task. The little craft flew over the water. Jan took the rudder, directing their movements. Harry crawled to the bow, where he crouched, calling hysterically from time to time:—

"Here it comes. It is on top of us. No! Yes! We are doomed!"

It was like the repetition of a silly song. Jan fastened his eyes on the object of their terror, watching the crumbling pieces that fell from it with loud reports into the sea. So they rode on the waves for a time that, measured by seconds, was short, but, from the beating of their frightened hearts, seemed to stretch out into eternity.

A sound rent the air that was like the bellowing of a hundred cannon. The boat was lifted from the water, as if a volcano had burst forth beneath the sea. One side of the iceberg, thousands of tons in weight, had split from the rest and dropped into the ocean. They were carried up — it seemed to the very sky. They fell, boat and men, back into the gulfing waves.

A tremendous sea was raised. White crests, set on green slopes of water, tore after the rushing mountain in its progress. The vessel was smashed, between water and ice, into infinitesimal fragments, which were hurled to the winds and away.

Giles knew nothing more for a time after that instant when he was propelled, like a shot from a gun, out into the air. He came to his senses with a feeling of intense, creeping cold; not the drowsiness that comes from freezing, but the sharp ache that precedes it. He recovered his wits with a shudder. He was lying upon a floe of ice. The tumult was subsiding, yet the violence of the waves was still such that the ice about him was rocked by its force. He heard ominous cracks in all directions. He sprang upright, peering about him for a sight of the others. Nothing was to be seen but water, ice, and sky.

He looked for a safer foothold. Another floating expanse was unbroken and promised comparative security. He could see the remnants of the berg plunging about in the distance, its balance disturbed by the crash. Masses broke from its sides: the roar of their fall was carried across the waves. A mist shrouded the awful view. Giles listened and looked, bent double in his abstracted search for sign of his comrades.

What was that to the south?

He sprang over one fragment of ice to another, gazing back and forth, first at that uncertain southern line that he dared not name, even to himself, then at his feet to guard his steps. There was cause for caution. The least misstep in these movements from one swaying piece to another would mean death by drowning or by being ground to bits in the ice.

The line to the south became more and more distinct. It was the rocky coast of the land. Giles took another survey of his surroundings. He felt that he could not try to reach the shore until every doubt was removed as to the others' fate. Far to his right, upon another floating cake, he made out faintly a black speck against the white. It was not a seabird stopped to rest, for it did not move. He made his tedious, difficult way in its direction. The water became calmer; passage over the crevices was less difficult, although far from easy. The speck grew to the shape of a man, and he hastened on. It never stirred. Finally, Giles began to call at the top of his lungs.

Were any of the three — Hudson, Harry, or Jan — saved too, he might know by this halloo that there was another survivor. They might seek each other until they came together. He shrieked their names out into the terrible desolation. No answering cry came to him. But the figure moved. He saw a man stagger to an upright position. He came closer. The man shaded his eyes with one hand. The sun dispersed the mist, shining fully into Giles's face. For a moment everything was black before him. He gave a sob of thanksgiving, for he had recognized Jan.

The two friends rushed together heedless of the perilous path, of everything save that they had found one another again. They fell on their knees, with a prayer of gratitude upon their lips. Neither knew anything of Hudson nor of his son: from that day to this their fate has been a mystery. It is almost certain that they were swallowed up in the waves, but no man saw them die. Jan had struggled from the water to the ice only to be again tossed off it by another mighty wave. His head was badly cut and he must have fainted, when he once more climbed up on the floe. He said Giles's shout came to him from out a sweet dream of home. He opened his eyes to the hard realities that faced them.

It was a long tramp, and they were scarcely equal to it, over the broken ice to that which stretched out from the shore. At length they reached it, crossed slowly its glassy surface, climbed along the rough scraps that were piled up next the beach, then to the rocks beyond, and finally came to a patch of moss upon which they fell, exhausted.

They were ashore upon a barren plateau between a small hill and a tall, black cliff. The wind raged pitilessly across the ice. The cold, dark water chilled their wet bodies to the bone. Snow drifted through the ravine. Yet the sun was warm, and this snow was only brought upon the tempest. It was summer after all, though an Arctic summer. They felt that, now they had arrived at dry land and were reunited, they should not despair whatever befell them.

"The first thing is to make a fire," observed Giles. "And the second is to find something to eat."

"I think the second comes first," suggested Jan. "Cold though I am, I am hungry, too, and I see a bird's nest in a fissure of the rocks. What do you say to a half dozen eggs? They will give us strength to discuss our further proceedings."

The eggs were gathered and swallowed. Then they sat down to strike a light from their knives and a bit of flint. Stunted willows grew along the stream that found the ocean here. They pulled the fluff from the downy blossoms and made a little pile. Over this they worked until spark after spark had fallen and ignited. They fed the flash to a blaze with tendrils of dry moss. At last they had a fire.

CHAPTER XXIX

FROM BAY TO RIVER

THEY sat by the roaring fire, drying their drenched clothing and talking over the future.

"We must get to the south," said Giles. "And still, how are we to make the journey? We have no arms except our knives; no food, nor any method of transporting it. The days will soon be shortening. Do you suppose that it would be possible for us to reach a settlement, either of Indians or of French traders, before winter?"

"No," answered Jan candidly. "I am afraid it is out of the question. I should think the best thing we could do would be to build a hut here, where we have the materials; to lay in provisions, and make ourselves knapsacks of sealskin for next spring's march. We should be able to smoke and salt some food, perhaps sufficient, with what we could fish and trap along the route, — I take for granted we would follow the stream as far as we could, — to keep us from actual starvation until we fell in with some human beings."

It was not a brilliant prospect, yet it was distinctly the best plan that they could make. Their hearts sank at the notion of at least four months of total darkness, buried in this dreary land. However, they said nothing to dispirit one another, and set to work diligently while they had light to pursue their tasks. They took a survey of their surroundings, finding very little vegetation, — a few small, pale flowers, and patches of moss and grass, a waste of jagged rocks, and the high, frowning cliffs. The willows were of the dwarf variety, the trunk not larger than a lead pencil, the slender branches trailing upon the earth. A dry-leaved plant that grew among the rocks, a sort of heather, furnished them with part of their fuel. Moreover, the beds of dried moss were practically inexhaustible, for their depth was beyond all discovering. This was material for a blaze rather than a steady, glowing heat. There was a dead seal upon the beach, and a narwhal was cast up on the ice within walking distance, not long after the boys' arrival here. The blubber, no less than the meat and skin, was so necessary to them that they lost no time in hacking and cutting — it was slow, hard work — the two bodies into pieces for their future use.

They were bothered by foxes that hung about the place, on the watch for something to seize and carry off. One of the boys was always on guard beside the meat until they could dissever it and carry it into the stone hut they built, cementing the rocks with mud and moss. Against the only opening was placed a slab, too heavy to be rolled away by anything not gifted with hands.

They caught a number of ducks by a spring trap that Jan constructed of loose stones among the rocks. The narwhal and the seal produced an enormous heap of blubber. The boys were obliged to store cakes of ice with it, lest it spoil before winter came. They had quantities of seal meat, and many birds that were laid away with the fat. They saw that they need not fear for the immediate future. The preparation of food for their journey was the most pressing need, after both storehouse and hut for themselves had been erected from the rocks and stones.

Many a time the two boys remembered those words of Prince Maurice: that no sort of useful knowledge was superfluous to a pioneer. The information they had gathered by their glimpses of Indian and Esquimau life, and their experiences during the past winter with Hudson, all came into play. They made vessels of soapstone, and lined them with dry moss, pouring oil over that. They constructed a tunnel to their new home, pinning duckskins together with bits of bone to make a curtain at the entrance.

There is always a pleasure in surmounting difficulties. It was not the dull winter that they had dreaded. They used to laugh together over their triumphs or their failures; they found something to do each day, and they looked for spring and talked of home as hopefully as if no doubt lurked in either mind that the nearing expedition would prove successful.

Then the sunshine appeared, growing longer and stronger every day. There must be haste now. The boys turned their backs upon this shelter, not without some homesickness for the safety it afforded. Their equipment was crude. They carried skin bags, filled with strips of preserved meats, on their shoulders. They had bows and arrows of flexible bone strung with sinews of the narwhal, fish-lines and hooks of the same manufacture; they owned their knives, and Giles, the narwhal's horn, Jan, a sort of spear they had fashioned by lashing bits of bone together.

They kept along the river bank, sleeping wherever their strength gave out, and they found they could make no further progress for the time. But they pushed endurance to its utmost limits. If they were overtaken by the winter night, they knew that this would be the last sun they should ever see. They caught some fish. They shot a few birds with their improvised arrows; and sometimes the trap, which they invariably set before they went to sleep, was found to contain a captive when they woke. The long march was not so terrible to face as it had been in anticipation. Water never failed them in that region of lakes and rivers. They were guided by the sound, and kept strictly to the course of some stream.

One day an arrow whistled past their ears as they were skirting a thickly wooded island out in the river that now led them south. They stood still to hearken. The splash of a distant paddle was heard. They saw nothing; there was no further sound.

"We are getting into the region of human life," said Jan. "I should think it might welcome us more kindly. We must be on the lookout henceforth, Giles, for Indian foes."

"Or friends," was the comment. "If we should fall in with any Algonquins like those on the river Hudson discovered, I should expect Winona's totem to help us. But it is not agreeable, is it, to walk in constant fear of an arrow better aimed than by yonder archer."

They were not molested again in any manner during that day nor the next. Then they entered a great forest, the first they had encountered, although trees had become more abundant for some time past. There was a well-defined path to lead them. The pines sighed through the waving branches. The day was overcast. The clouded sun did not affect the solemn shadows of this vast wood.

A long-drawn, unearthly wail broke the stillness. It was like nothing human. It seemed the cry of a lost soul.

"That was no wild beast!" said Giles.

"Hush! I hear footsteps."

They drew aside into the underbrush. A thicket hid them from sight. They could now see a long line of men advancing. The procession bore litters, on which motionless forms were stretched under coverings of fur. Some of them carried bundles swung over their backs. At intervals the same long, low cry they had heard before was uttered.

"Shall we join them?" muttered Giles.

Jan's face indicated indecision. It appeared to be safest to keep out of sight and let them pass without parley. The following morning they met another such party, and another that afternoon. When it lost its first weirdness, they grew bolder. Stepping out from their hiding-place, they addressed the foremost men by propitiatory gestures.

The Indians looked surprised, although not so shocked as those whom the Half Moon had found. These were accustomed to white men from traditions of the fishing-boats along the coast, while some of them had seen the traders at their posts. They consulted together, pointing to the two youths, gesticulating wildly, though whether in friendship or enmity the boys could not decide. Finally one of them approached the strangers, his companions on the alert for any sign of bad faith. He spoke to them in French.

Jan's face glowed with pleasure. They could assuredly prove their innocent intentions if they could make themselves understood. He told their story rapidly. The Indian shook his head. He was no adept in the foreign tongue. Jan repeated his statement very slowly, using only a few and simple words. The man smiled, wheeled about, and retailed what he had heard. There was a further discussion.

Then the interpreter announced their decision. The white men could accompany them; afterwards they would be carried back to the great river — the St. Lawrence — and sent to the fort that Champlain had established near what is now Quebec. This they would do if, for their part, Jan and Giles would turn over to them their knives and bows and spears. They were to be quite unarmed.

It was an appalling risk, yet there appeared to be no alternative. They consulted together. These were Hurons, perhaps at war with Winona's people. It might harm their interests, rather than advance them, to show the Algonquin's stone. They were placing their lives absolutely in the Indians' power. Still, after all, they were at their mercy, with no fighting strength, if they kept their weapons. So they surrendered what they carried, and took their place beside the interpreter in the ranks.

The procession moved on, while he told its purpose to the boys. The dead of the four nations, after a funeral service, were laid upon a scaffold, or, occasionally, in a temporary grave. Every ten or twelve years the bodies were gathered together and conveyed to a common sepulchre. They were upon their way to the meeting place, Ossossané, the chief village of the Hurons.

Finally they emerged upon the spot, a clearing of several acres in the pine forest that swept to the borders of Nottawassaga Bay. The town lay at a little distance on the bank of the water. It consisted of a number of bark houses, well constructed, and now filled with visitors. Fires gleamed through the trees. Maidens and youths were shooting at a target for prizes the mourners offered in the name of the dead.

The bags of bones or the bodies which had been borne on the litters were suspended from the rafters in the houses. Some of them were done up in rolls, decorated with beads and feathers. These were taken down when the day of burial came, and were lamented over by the women, the awful screams — supposed to imitate the farewell of the departing soul — resounding through the woods.

Processions were re-formed. Each carried its own dead to a place appointed for it on the outskirts of the clearing. The bodies were placed upon the ground. Funeral gifts, many of them the richest furs, were spread out to be examined and admired. Fires were lighted, and food was cooked. It was the most uncanny of festivals. As the sun declined, the gifts were rolled into packages, the bodies were lifted to the bearers' shoulders.

A chief gave a signal. The throng pressed forward from every side to a scaffolding in the midst of the clearing. On this were fastened many upright and cross poles. Underneath it yawned a wide, deep grave. The Indians swarmed up the ladders to the platform. Chiefs standing on it called to the crowd praises of the dead, and of the gifts now being busily hung upon the poles. Men were lining the pit with beaver skins. A number of large copper kettles were set on these. A hideous scene ensued.

There were a dozen Indians standing in this long grave. The bodies were thrown in to them, while they arranged them in orderly rows by the assistance of long poles. Those on the brink cast them down out of their fur wrappings in showers of rattling bones. Horrible cries attended the ceremony; and around immense fires danced the wild red figures like demons in a nightmare.

CHAPTER XXX

YOUNG AMERICANS

It was hard to believe that at such a time and place the two unarmed white men were safe, yet they met nothing save kind usage. After this disgusting orgy was over, they were conducted quietly and peaceably to the river, as had been agreed.

The interpreter still attended them. On their journey to the St. Lawrence they were present at a feast given by a village through which they passed, in honor of the assembled chiefs, dispersing after the burial services. The large bark house was full of guests, seated upon furs spread over the ground. Each visitor as he entered gave a grunt of salute; each carried his own spoon and wooden dish. The host served the feast, of which it was not thought courteous for him to have a share. The company thrust forward their wooden dishes to be filled in turn. First came boiled, pounded corn, with bits of fish and flesh unsalted. Broiled meats of various kinds were next set forth, and proved very palatable. The white visitors were treated exactly as were the others. The boys quite enjoyed the glimpse of savage hospitality.

They found canoes at the shore of the river. In these they embarked for a voyage to Champlain's fort. It was an enchanting trip, past forests gay with vines turning red with the coming autumn, past solid walls of green, over the clear blue water of the mighty stream. By and by the buildings came into sight that the great discoverer had raised four years ago. A wooden wall, topped by a gallery with loopholes for guns, ran around three inner houses and a courtyard, from one side of which a tall dovecot arose. The whole was encompassed by a moat. Several small cannon stood on the platform, pointed towards the St. Lawrence. A large storehouse joined the fort, and a garden was laid out near by, stripped of its fruits, for summer was over. Champlain himself came to meet his guests. He was a round-faced, stout man, with the penetrating glance of one accustomed to peril and to relying upon observation and quick reflection. He had made several voyages to France in the past few years, but this season, fortunately, he had omitted the excursion.

They were made heartily welcome. It appeared that he knew M. Chapelain, and of course had heard of Hudson's expedition. He gave such gifts to their guide as the man demanded, dismissing him well pleased.

"Now what are we to do with you?" asked the Frenchman.

"Our dearest hope," said Giles, "is to become American colonists."

"You have not had enough of it, with what you have undergone?"

"No, sir," they cried with one voice. "We only ask for another chance."

"I would not advise you to stay here with me," said Champlain, frowning, "nor at Port Royal in Acadia, although I can send you thither. Matters here are sadly unsettled. Then, if you have friends in France, you naturally would wish to return to them for a season, to assure them of your welfare. I should advise your return in the next vessel that comes from home to the Port."

"It was our own thought, sir," said Giles. "Then we can make a fresh start to some one of the colonies."

"You are two gallant youths," the older

man remarked, with a knowing smile. "Surely it will be your own fault if you return to America alone."

Giles blushed. "Jan's sister"—he began.

Champlain laughed, yet his eyes were moist.

"Yours is a beautiful friendship," he cried, "like that of David and Jonathan. You even look for a closer bond between you. I trust you may be brothers, according to your hope."

They were given over to other guides by their good host, and before the winter came arrived at the Acadian colony, flourishing a few years before, but now reduced to a famished state that found it hard to greet joyfully any addition to their number. Fortunately the new arrivals brought food with them, but the winter was long and severe. No ship arrived from France with succor: they were reduced to piteous straits. On a fair May day the long anticipated vessel from home appeared. Captain Fleury found only five men at Port Royal, the rest being scattered about the woods searching for roots and fishing in the streams. He replenished the lean larder, took the two priests of the settlement on board with him, and invited our heroes to accompany him and his chief, La Saussaye, on a further cruise to establish a settlement.

The boys accepted delightedly. They sailed on along the coast. A fog arose, in which they suffered extreme terrors, every instant dreading the crash upon a deadly reef. The following morning saw a bright sun shining upon the ship as it entered the waters known as Frenchman's Bay, upon the coast of Maine.

The sailors clamored for a hearing in regard to the terms of their engagement. The priests stilled the dispute by leading them all ashore, where mass was celebrated and a cross raised on the headland. Father Biard went away to the woods to visit a great Indian chief, Asticon, who sent for him. He found a new spot for a settlement, and returned with news of it to the others.

The ship was brought here and the colonists were landed. They raised a cross; then they proposed building a fort. La Saussaye was determined to dig ground and sow crops at once. They were in the midst of a quarrel, when a warning shout from the beach called them away from their troubles, and they flocked down to the shore.

A vessel was approaching the land at all

speed. The decks were thronged with men. Seven cannon projected from either side. Red flags waved from masthead and stern. It was an English smuggling bark, under the command of Samuel Argall, lately busying himself in the affairs of the Jamestown colony. He had, this same spring, captured the Indian princess Pocahontas and carried her to Jamestown, where she was wooed and wed by Master Rolfe. His present errand was to expel the French from any settlements in the limits of King James's patents. He was sent out by the governor of Virginia, and led by an Indian whom he had picked up in Penobscot Bay.

Everything was confusion among the settlers. Their pilot ran away and hid among the islands. La Saussaye was completely at a loss for advice. Fleury, a priest, three of the under officers, Giles, and Jan hurried to the ship. They endeavored to cast loose her cables, but Argall was too quick for them.

A volley of cannon boomed out, while drums and trumpets sounded through the din. "Fire!" called the captain.

Giles sprang to one gun, Jan to another. The Englishman was intercepted by that brave priest, Du Thet, who was first at the muzzle and fired, but without taking aim. There was no avail in pursuing what was not a combat, but carnage. The English boarded the vessel, its scanty crew every one wounded. Du Thet was dead. They landed, demanded an interview with the colony's commander, and asked for his royal letters and commissions. La Saussaye was not able to produce them, for the best of reasons. He had fled to the woods at the approach of Argall, and that crafty fellow improved his absence by ransacking the chests in the Frenchman's tent, removing such papers as he selected.

His play at courtesy vanished when La Saussaye admitted that he could not show his commissions. He and fourteen others of the colonists were set adrift in an open boat. In the course of time, after many vicissitudes, they crossed the Bay of Fundy, rounded Cape Sable, and on the coast of Nova Scotia found two French traders which bore them back to France.

The remaining fourteen men were conveyed on board Argall's ship. Father Biard said something in an undertone to the captain when Giles, his head bandaged, followed by Jan, whose arm was in a sling, came upon deck. Argall walked up to them.

"Art thou an Englishman?" he demanded.

"Yes," said Giles. "And my friend here is Dutch."

Argall grew very red as he saw what he had done. "How came ye in such company?" he questioned sullenly.

"Because they gave shelter and food to two starving wayfarers," was Giles's defiant answer.

"What meanst thou?"

He told the outlines of their three-years' voyage.

"Hudson!" exclaimed the smuggler. "'T was he discovered the river to the southwest of us."

"Ay. We were on the Half Moon with him."

"Is 't so? There is a Dutch trading fort established on the island at its mouth. Knew ye aught of that?"

Giles shook his head.

"I am bound for Virginia," their captor proceeded to explain. "An it please ye, we can drop you there upon our way. Mayhap ye would relish it rather than further voyage with us."

They understood this for a shame-faced attempt towards restitution for their misuse.

They assented to the proposition; not long afterwards it was carried out.

On a lovely summer day they again entered the noble bay from which their unfortunate leader had looked forth upon the island of a future metropolis. Four houses stood where the city of New York greets the traveler to-day. All trace of Winona and her wandering tribe had disappeared. Yet in the future Giles more than once found that the totem she had given him served to make allies for him among the Indians.

A ship soon came out from Holland which took the two aboard. After forty-two months of wandering they set foot once more upon European soil. They stopped at Portsmouth to give poor Mistress Hudson their sad tidings and then hastened on to France. Public and private news awaited them. Prince Henry of England was dead. Giles's country was unquiet as ever. Holland was struggling out from under its long pressure of strife. Germany was torn by those dissensions which should culminate but shortly in the Thirty-Years' War. France was suffering from that disordered state that characterized the regency. M. Chapelain, who long ago so feared the plague, had fallen a victim to it in the previous autumn. His widow, Dame Tryon, and the young girls greeted with rapture the adventurers they had given up for lost.

The remnant of Hudson's crew, after enduring untold agonies, had been taken on board a fishing-vessel and brought to land. The youths never sought to see any of them again.

Preparations were speedily completed for leaving a country that had nothing more to offer to any one of them. Even Mme. Chapelain and Nurse Janet were glad to accompany Meg and Jan and Giles, while Annemie became Mistress Valentine the day before the vessel sailed from port.

They had selected port Manhattan, on Hudson's River, for their future home. The ship entered the harbor at sunset one fair day. Giles pointed the site of their new fortunes to his young wife and to his sister.

"'T is a goodly and a pleasant land,'" he quoted Hudson's words.

"And henceforth," added Jan, "we are neither English, Dutch, nor French. From this hour, thank God, we may call ourselves Americans."

www.ingramcontent.com/pod-product-compliance
Lightning Source LLC
Chambersburg PA
CBHW031852220426
43663CB00006B/586